HANDBOOK OF ZEBRA FINCHES

DR. MATTHEW M. VRIENDS

Pictorial Credits:
Front Cover: Gunter Oppenborn
Color: Paul Kwast: 181, 184, 185, 188, 189; Harry V. Lacey, 192;
Gunter Oppenborn, 65, 68, 69, 72, 73, 76, 77, 80, 81, 84, 85, 92,
93, 96, 161, 164, 165, 168, 169; R.A. Vowles, 88; Dr. Matthew M.
Vriends, 172, 173, 176, 177, 180; S.D. Wilson, 89.
Black and White: Dr. Herbert R. Axelrod, 114; Harry V. Lacey,
1, 6, 8, 11, 12, 14, 17, 18, 19, 21, 23, 26, 29, 30, 32, 34, 38, 44, 46,
50, 52, 54, 56, 58, 61, 64, 66, 70, 74, 78, 82, 86 (below), 90 (top),
94, 101, 103, 104, 110, 118, 124, 126, 130, 140, 144, 145, 147,
150, 152, 153, 154, 156, 157, 158, 163, 166, 174, 178, 179, 182,
183, 186, 187, 190, 191, 193, 194, 196, 198, 199, 201, 202, 203,
204, 205, 208, 209, 211, 212, 213, 215, 216, 221, 223, 225, 227,
228, 229, 231, 232, 234, 236, 238, 239, 240, 243, 244, 245, 246,
247, 249; Louise van der Meid, 37, 86 (top), 90 (below), 97, 98,
99, 109, 120, 125, 128, 132, 137, 138, 146, 148, 170, 207, 235;
Cyril and Maud Wilkinson, 40.
Line Drawings: Paxton Chadwick.

ISBN 0-87666-886-4

Distributed in the U.S. by T.F.H. Publications, Inc., 211 West
Sylvania Avenue, PO Box 427, Neptune, NJ 07753; in England by
T.F.H. (Gt. Britain) Ltd., 13 Nutley Lane, Reigate, Surrey; in Canada
to the book store and library trade by Beaverbooks Ltd., 150 Lesmill
Road, Don Mills, Ontario M38 2T5, Canada; in Canada to the pet
trade by Rolf C. Hagen Ltd., 3225 Sartelon Street, Montreal 382,
Quebec; in Southeast Asia by Y.W. Ong, 9 Lorong 36 Geylang,
Singapore 14; in Australia and the South Pacific by Pet Imports Pty.
Ltd., P.O. Box 149, Brookvale 2100, N.S.W. Australia; in the British
Crown Colony of Hong Kong, in South Africa by Valid Agencies,
P.O. Box 51901, Randburg 2125 South Africa. Published by T.F.H.
Publications, Inc., Ltd.

Contents

"Soyons fidèles à nos faiblesses"
for Lucy, Tanya,
Kees and Kitty

Zebra finches can be kept in cages or aviaries, both indoors and out. Outdoor aviaries are by far the most satisfactory, and every fancier ought to try and find room in his garden for at least one small aviary.

Preface

The object of this book is to discuss in simple terms the many phases of the fascinating hobby of keeping and breeding zebra finches, plus to mention a few of the other lovely and lively birds that can be kept with them in the same aviary. The information presented in this book has been gained through many years of experience in breeding all types of finches and also from much research work. I have called on every possible resource available in order to make this book not only authoritative but also interesting enough to warrant its being read and enjoyed by both the beginner and the experienced aviculturist.

Most of all, I want the reader to know that the keeping of a single pair of zebra finches in a large cage for their song or color, or the keeping of several pairs for breeding, is not a difficult task and there isn't any magic connected with it. Anyone may enjoy the somewhat strange song of the zebra finch and even more the beauty of these charming birds if he is willing to devote only a small portion of his time to keeping the birds happy and contented. I would like to thank Mrs. Naomi Greenberg and my wife, Mrs. Lucy Vriends-Parent, for their invaluable assistance in the preparation of this edition.

Dr. Matthew M. Vriends

Finches are seldom kept permanently in cages these days. Although they live and appear quite happy in cages of generous size, they are far more interesting in an aviary.

I. ZEBRA FINCHES AND THEIR CARE

Chapter 1. Zebra Finches In General

Introduction

Zebra finches are undoubtedly among the most popular aviary birds we have today. They are particularly well suited for anyone just beginning to keep birds, for they demand little in the way of care, have a bright and vigorous song and are easy to bred. But finches can also win the hearts of experienced bird breeders because they offer endless opportunities to achieve fascinating color variety through breeding experimentation. The zebra finch is indeed a bird that gives everyone pleasure.

In both national and international journals published over the past few years, one can read about the enormous development that has been made, and continues to be made, in the breeding of finches. Breeders are constantly experimenting to perfect color and form, and they are even attempting to see what happens when they cross the finch with the other breeds of birds. As in all hobbies, there are also popular fads in bird raising, and the breeder should be aware of these trends. As you can see, the zebra finch offers such challenge and variety that I believe it is worthwhile to tell more about these "Australian sparrows" or "brown-eared finches," as they are also called.

For a long time the zebra finch and many other so-called "weaver finches" were placed in the subfamily Estrildinae of the family of the real weavers (Ploceidae), but this classification was changed when it became apparent that there were enormous differences in anatomical structure, feather markings and behavior patterns between zebra finches and real weavers. Even on ecological grounds, the classification could not be justified. At the moment, zebra finches are considered to belong to the family Estrildidae. This shifting of family relationships becomes even more logical when one observes the method of nest-building. Real weavers invariably begin by weaving a few blades of grass or stems around a branch; after that, a ring-shaped structure is formed that serves as the sides. When the birds have completed this, they build the roof. It is only after the entire outside structure is completed that attention is given to the making of the brooding area. For estrildids the method of nest-building is totally different. First, a dish-like construction is built in the fork of a branch, followed by the sides and roof. Real "weavers" never build in such a manner! Consequently, the name "weaver finch" is a source of confusion and it would be far better to regard them as "grass finches" (Erythrini), since this group lives primarily on grass seeds and builds its nest from blades of grass.

Over the years the scientific name of the zebra finch has also undergone a number of changes. In spite of the fact that in Australia only one variety of zebra finch is found, a number of ornithologists commonly described color deviations found in particular areas. This led to the inclusion in the literature of anywhere from three to seven subspecies. However, Keast showed that in Australia there exist no varieties of zebra finches, no matter how improbable that may sound. The absence of subspecies in so enormous an area is associated with the fact that the yearly drought in central Australia forces the birds to seek new watering places and in the process acts as an inducement for them to mix with birds from other areas.

If we accept that there are no geographically differentiated varieties, then we can understand the frequently given scientific designation *Taeniopygia guttata castanotis* (Gould 1837). The forms *hartogi* (1920), *mouki* (1912), *alexandrae* (1912), *mungi* (1912), *wayensis* (1912) and *roebuki* (1913), as described by G.M. Mathews in his 12-volume work, *The Birds of Australia* (London 1910-1927), must then also be looked

10

There are many zebra finch colors. These colors are becoming more readily available all the time.

The male zebra finch has a large oval patch of bright rust-red bordered on the front side by a fine line of black which starts at the eyes, giving a tear-stained effect.

upon as synonyms for *castanotis*. This certainly does not mean that one will not find in his own research differences between zebra finches. Indeed, there is great variety in size, color of bill and breast markings.

A separate variety is found on Timor and several other Sunda islands: Letti, Sermatta, Luang and Moa. The color of this zebra finch is a brownish yellow, and the top and back of the head are darker than in the Australian variety. Females from Timor have a darker back and breast than those from Australia. Therefore, the conclusions reached by the ornithologist Delacour are incorrect when, as an outgrowth of his research on Flores and Timor, he no longer accepts the fact that all zebra finches, including those from Australia, are the same. He prefers to include them with the mannikins and munias (Amadinae) instead of grass finches. He gives the Australian zebra finch the scientific name of *Poephila guttata castanotis,* and the Timor birds *Poephila guttata guttata. Poephila* (Gr.) means "lover of grass," *guttata* (Lat.) means "droplet markings" and *castanotis* (Gr.) refers to the "chestnut-brown ear." If we leaf through the pages of a modern book on birds we almost always find *Poephila castanotis*.

For all that, it is apparent that scientific names most certainly have their use and function and often reflect particular characteristics and qualities of plants and animals. The common names, such as those found in Dutch, French, English and German, are frequently a thorn in the side of the biologist. It is not unusual to find a locally-given name that is identical to a name used elsewhere but referring to two totally different plants or animals. I can best illustrate the difficulties encountered by giving an example. In the Netherlands, there lives in the extensive reed marshes the bearded tit, known scientifically as *Panurus biarmicus*. This titmouse has absolutely no relationship to the bearded tit from Southwest Africa, which has the rather dignified name of *Sporopipes squamifrons* and is a type of weaver. Therefore, a bit of advice: stick with the scientific name!

Important Information
Scientific name: In spite of what has been written above: *Poephila castanotis*.
English: Zebra finch, sometimes called "chestnut-eared finch," "Australian sparrow," and "brown-eared finch."
Dutch: Zebravink; less often, bruinoorvink.
French: Diamant mandarin, zébré Australien, moineau mandarin or diamant zébré.
Danish: Zebra fink.
German: Zebra fink.
Swedish: Zebra fink.
Size: Length 10 - 10.5 cm; tail 3.5 cm; wings 5.3 cm.
Color of male (in the wild): Grey-blue head and neck; drab grey-brown back; dark grey-brown wings; blue-grey chest with black wavy markings; the lower part of the chest is

black; sides orange-red with round white spots; belly beige-white; tail black with white diagonal bands; white "moustache"; orange-red ear spot; under the eye a black band marking the front edge of the ear spot; red eyes; deep red beak and yellow-brown feet.

Color of female (in the wild): Light grey above; grey or sometimes almost white ear spot; grey throat, neck, chest and sides. All the other parts are very similar to the male.

It is interesting to see the difference in color between the grey zebra finches of the wild and those that have been bred for generations in captivity. The eyes of those raised in an aviary are dark brown and the head color is ash-brown, while those living in the wild have a drab greyish brown color. The underside of the wild female is almost as white as that of the male; the domesticated females are generally pale creamy or brownish yellow.

The original Australian color variety is the gray zebra finch. In all varieties now available, the size of the zebra is four inches including the tail of one and one-fourth inches.

Color of the young: Same as that of the female, only the black and white head markings are missing. The underside of the body is creamy brown-yellow, and the beak is black.

Habitat: The zebra finch, one of the most common of all the Australian grass finches, lives all over Australia (except in wet sclerophyll forests) and behaves differently from one area to another. In northern Australia it is found mostly in little trees and bushes in overgrown grassland as well as in the open savannah. In central Australia it is often found in rugged, coarse plants (called "mulga" by the natives) which require little water. It is also found in areas where spinifex, a coarse grass with twisted blades, grows. Here the zebra finch looks for young trees and shrubs in which to conceal itself or build a nest.

Everything points to the fact that since the earliest colonization the number of zebra finches in these dry areas has sharply increased because of the building of sewage systems, watertanks and watering places for live stock. In the thickly populated areas of eastern, southeastern and southwestern Australia these birds are a familiar sight around houses, parks, gardens, orchards and meadows with wooded groves. Zebra finches in the wild are on the whole not shy, but they never become as trusting and familar as, for example, the Sydney or thorn finches or Bicheno finch. They never come and sit on a window sill or balcony, for example. In places where there is no water one will look in vain for the zebra finch, which accounts for the fact that it is so rarely seen in northern and central Australia. It stays mostly on the ground, where it hops about on both feet at the same time, much like our house sparrow.

Food: This consists primarily of ripe and half-ripe grass seeds, although insects are taken, too. Often finches can be seen chasing flying termites and other small insects that move through the air, and on the ground among the leaves they know where the insects hide. They can also be observed springing from the ground into the air to seize windborne grass seeds. Finches drink the way pigeons do, sucking up the water rather than scooping it like chickens. In the wild I have seen zebra finches drinking in the company of other kinds of birds, such as diamond doves *(Geopelia cuneata)*, cockatiels *(Nymphicus hollandicus)* and budgerigars *(Melopsittacus undulatus)*.

Voice: 1. If the birds are in high spirits and have enough food, they let out a loud trumpet-like "tie-tie-tie." This is heard when they move in massive flights from one area to another. If a few birds drop out of the flock, a louder, more urgent "tie-tie" can be heard which may well be a cry of distress. The same call is heard when the birds warn one another of impending danger.

2. When they are in flight and wish to maintain contact with others of the same breed, they give out a low "tit-tit" which can be heard incessantly among very large flocks serving as a sort of communication call. The same call is also used upon other occasions, such as during pairing. At this time the call comes very rapidly and sounds as though it were thrust out in pain. This sound is also noted when a male wishes to call the attention of his spouse to a well-situated nesting place, but then the sound is higher in pitch.

3. When zebra finches are chasing each other there is a resounding and often aggressive "wssst," which has been aptly compared with "the tearing of a piece of cotton."

4. The real song consists of low trills and a loud "tie-tie" call. Each song phase is repeated several times, practically without variation. Only wild birds alternate this song with the communication call mentioned earlier.

Zebra finches in captivity are known for their typical "trumpeting," but this well-known call is not typical of wild birds. Only the males sing their song at great length, and it can probably be thought of as an expression of contentment. Singing in the natural state can most often be heard when the little birds are alone, and it most frequently occurs after

16

Despite the fact that zebra finches leave the bird fancier rather frustrated with their tendency to over-produce, they are joyful and amusing birds with a very pleasant appearance.

mating.

Mating: With practically all grass finches it is the habit of the male, during display or the so-called mating dance, to hold a blade of grass, a straw or a feather in his beak. This is never done by zebra finches.

Immelmann writes of the display: "During the introductory phase the male and female jump up and down between two branches rubbing their beaks over and over again, their tails directed at each other, going up and down. After much hopping, the female stops and the male moves toward her along the branch in a rhythmic, turning dance while his feet and body rotate with each jump, all this being accompanied by an incessant song. During the display the tail is pointed toward the female and the crown feathers lie flat on the top of the head; the feathers from the back of the head and cheeks stand straight upright making the black and white colored portions of the head and the chestnut-brown cheeks

Besides oval patches the male zebra has fine zebra-like bars of black and grayish white extending from the chin to the chest and becoming bolder at the chest. The sides of the chest and flanks have a broad band of bright chestnut spangled with prominent white spots.

The female is drab by comparison with the male and lacks the zebra markings on the chest, the chestnut and white flanks and the rust-red cheek patches.

sharply accented; the white belly feathers are also expanded. All this is devised to make an enormous impact upon the female. When the male makes his way along the branch to the female she begins to move her tail up and down and joins him in fluttering, where upon the mating takes place."

The zebra finch comes rapidly into breeding condition after rain at any time of the year, but mainly in May. With zebra finches in captivity we see very much the same display. The dance and the mating can occur several times in succession. After the mating the male places himself in a horizontal position and makes an up and down vibrating motion with his tail corresponding with the behavior of the female. It is because of this that Morris speaks of "pseudo-female behavior." As a rule, the displays take place in small dead trees or brush, since the leaves of live vegetation hinder the birds in their motions. They are also known to mate on the ground or on rocks.

Even though birds raised in captivity do not seem to concern themselves unduly about remaining with one mate, it is presumed by ornithologists that zebra finches in the wild pair for a lifetime. After mating, the pair lives together the entire year and even stays together when they join the huge flocks. One would expect this during the breeding season, but zebra finches maintain their relationship beyond the brooding time. Cozily they disappear into their nests and sleep as the evening shadows fall, but they also make use of the nest during the day to protect themselves from the hot rays of the sun.

Nest-building, eggs and young: Generally, nests can be found in low thorny bushes or young trees as well as wooded groves that stand partly in water. Less often, nests are built on the ground in clumps of grass, in tree holes or in rabbit holes. Mention is regularly made of unusual nesting places such as termite hills, the substructure of nests of birds of prey, nests of grass finches that were summarily shoved out, swallow nests, under roofs, in gutters, in holes in wooden fence poles and in sheds.

The nest is a construction of rough grass, upholstered inside with soft grass and bits of fruit fuzz. The actual egg cup is prepared with feathers, rabbit hair and sheep wool. In places where it is difficult to find grass, the outside is made of fine little twigs and roots. Nests built in such places as brushwood can be described as "bottle-shaped" with the entrance on the side. If the nest happens to be built in a hollow, the birds do not bother to build their own roof at all.

Outside of breeding season, nests are frequently built for playing and sleeping, but these nests generally have the tunnel-like "neck of the bottle" entrance missing. Old brood nests are also used as sleeping places.

The future nursery is built by both parents, but it is usually the male that collects and brings in the building materials while the female works them into the nest structure. It has been observed by Immelmann, however, that this is not

Zebras nest in a standard finch box using dried grasses, nesting hair and any feathers which happen to be available. The droppings of the young birds are not carried away but are 'plastered' against the walls of the nest.

always the case ("in central Australia I have seen both male and female dragging building materials"), and I, too, have observed the same in southwestern Australia and Queensland. Perhaps both birds toil at building a nest quickly so it can be completed by the time the rains come. Under normal conditions zebra finches take their time, and it may take as long as two weeks to get the "cradle" ready.

The breeding season occurs at different times in different parts of Australia, due to the fact that successful breeding is to a large extent dependent upon the rainfall. In central Australia the zebra finches begin their nest building with the first rains, independent of the time of year. As we all know, where rain falls there are generally plants, and where there are plants, there is food. Since it is possible that the rains will be of very short duration, the birds begin to build their nests as quickly as possible in order to breed and raise at least one brood. In areas of greater rainfall the "Australian sparrows" breed from October to April.

Next to the importance of rain, successful breeding is dependent upon the temperature. This can be easily observed in southwestern Australia. The winters bring too much rain to assure successful breeding, so nesting takes place in autumn and spring. In summer there is no rain, and in winter it is too cold. However, if rain should happen to fall in summer, then the birds begin to breed immediately. In other places, such as eastern Australia, zebra finches breed the entire year with the exception of June and July, November and December.

A total clutch of eggs can range from three to eight, but generally there are four, five or six. They are pale blue. The size is quite variable; Immelmann gives measurements of 9.8 mm x 13.8 mm and 11.6 x 16.1 mm, which comes out to an average of 10.7 mm x 14.95 mm. Serventy and Whitehall (*Birds of Western Australia*, 1951) averaged the size of 10 eggs as 10.6 mm x 15.2 mm, varying from 10.2 mm x 14.7 mm to 10.9 mm x 15.7 mm. Mr. F.L. Whitlock has recorded as many as 23 eggs in one nest, which, according to Serventy and Whitehall, was probably a composite clutch due to the scarcity of nesting sites.

Brooding begins after the fourth or fifth egg is laid. The male as well as the female broods, relieving one another after periods of two or three hours. They do not change places at the nest but, rather, a short distance away. This is probably done to lead possible enemies away from the actual nest. It is interesting to note that when the male returns to the nest he will often have a bit of grass, down or a feather in his beak, while to the best of my knowledge the female never does this. Apparently the male works the bit he brings back into the nest wall as a way of "relaxing." After twilight both partners go into the nest, but with the first light of day, the male leaves.

After 12 to 16 days the young hatch. It is not possible to give the exact length of the brooding time, since it is dependent upon many factors such as the intensity of brooding and

White zebras are bright white with outstanding contrasts in the orange feet and legs and the brighter beaks. There are no pattern markings to point out sex, but the male has a decidedly richer red shade in the beak than does the female.

the state of the weather.

Baby zebra finches just out of the egg are flesh colored and almost totally bare. By the time they are three days old their skin is already noticeably darker, and within a week it is black. Their beaks are also quite light in the beginning, but these, too, become black after about 12 days. The offspring are blind at hatching, but after eight to 10 days they open their eyes; at about the same time, their first feathers appear. For the first two or three days the babies are totally mute, but after that soft "tearing" sounds can be heard, the "begging call." With each passing day it becomes louder, more intense and shriller.

The food, brought in by both parents, consists of half-ripe seeds from grasses and other plants along with soft, non-brittle insects. After approximately three weeks, depending upon the availability of food, the weather and other factors, the offspring fly out of the nest. In the beginning the parents lead them back to the nest in the evening to sleep. It has also been observed that during the day the parents will entice the young into the nest to make sure they get something to eat, a phenomenon rarely seen among zebra finches raised in captivity.

The family relationship is maintained for a fair amount of time, the offspring returning to the "parental home" to sleep. When the parents begin to build a new nest for a new clutch of eggs, however, the time has come for the young ones to take off on their own, though some of them return regularly to the old nest which is no longer used as a breeding place.

Molting begins after two months and lasts from one month to six weeks. The beak begins to turn red and is fully colored after 10 weeks but is not yet the lovely red of the adult bird, remaining a bit lighter for a while.

Socialization: Zebra finches live a very social life. In the wild, outside of the breeding season, they can be seen in large flocks ranging from 40 to more than 100 birds! When the weather conditions and the food supply are good, the birds are content to remain in the same place the whole year, building their nests and disappearing into them with their partners each evening.

In areas where the probability of drought is great, such as central and northern Australia, zebra finches move in search of water. At such times flocks of hundreds and even thousands can be seen! In the breeding season they stay near one another, but never in great numbers, the colonies generally consisting of five to 30 couples. For the most part, each couple has its own tree or bush, but where suitable growth is sparse two or three nests can be found in one tree or sturdy bush. It was interesting to read that in 1948 the ornithologist Whitlock found in the Wiluna district 13 occupied nests in a large hakea bush, while McGilp in 1944 came across 21 occupied nests in an acacia tree near Oodnadatta.

Immelmann contends that members of such a colony have a strong mutual contact with each other and apparently recognize each other's calls. "Neighbors" can come to each other's nests, but strangers beware! Several times a day the whole colony goes off to a watering place to drink, bathe, pluck each other's feathers and do whatever else it is that birds enjoy doing. Sometimes the urge to socialize is so strong that they all come to the same spot to sing. This spot is generally in the middle of the colony, and the whole population joins in, usually during the late afternoon.

The white-headed nun *(Lonchura maja)* is not as readily available as zebras. The white is softly tinged with traces of brown on the crown, and the change from the white to the brown on the body is softly blended instead of sharply divided as in other nun species.

Chapter 2. Tips for the Bird Enthusiast

Zebra finches make no great demands, and if you give them normal care and avoid fads or eccentricities, they will certainly breed. They are very easily satisfied. For example, if they are not provided with a nesting box, they will immediately try to find some suitable spot of their own for the nest.

For the new breeder, the grey or "wild-colored" zebra finch is extremely attractive, and for many years it has been recognized that its sturdiness and relative cheapness make it an excellent bird with which to begin. It is somewhat different with birds bred for unusual colors and other mutations. These are less suited to withstand difficulties and can also be on the expensive side. The exceptions are the white and fawn-brown varieties, but even then you would be well advised to develop skill and experience with the normal grey variety first.

Know what you are buying! Get a pair of very healthy birds with good feathers and no evidence of deformities of beak or feet. Those that sit sleeping with their heads in their feathers all the time and breathe rapidly or those whose eyes are tearing are obviously not completely healthy.

An important distinguishing mark is the color of the sturdy, cone-shaped beak. In the male as well as the female, the bill is red, though the female's is less intense in color. A bill that is black or red with a black background indicates that the bird is a juvenile.

Naturally the bird must have attained full color before it can begin to breed, but birds that are too old are also unsuited for breeding. These "senior citizens" can be recognized by the color of the beak: it is red with a grey-white background and looks as though it has been smeared with plaster.

If you want a good or—better yet—the best standard bird for breeding and possibly exhibiting, then be aware of the following points:

a. Tail should have even black and white markings;
b. Back should be strong, only slightly bent and not too thin; and
c. Wings should be drawn up high and well closed.

The male must have good breast markings as well as vividly colored side stripes with round white spots lying evenly next to each other. It goes without saying that, if you wish to achieve success in bird breeding, you must work with the best available or at least good material. This is the basis for responsible breeding and reduces the chances of failure to a minimum.

It is not advisable to go out immediately and buy a great number of pairs, but instead limit yourself to the purchase of one, two or at the very most three pairs so you can devote yourself to them completely. In this way the most elementary aspects of caring for the birds, including providing proper housing, will not escape your notice. It is actually best to begin with one couple, but if you really want to keep two pairs there is nothing wrong as long as they are not placed together. Two couples give an incredible amount of trouble, so keep either one pair or three. Personally, I find three a bit too much.

For good breeding results the finches must be housed in a substantial cage or aviary. It is perfectly all right to keep other varieties of birds with them. As a matter of fact, when the others begin their mating dances or displays they stimulate the zebra finches to behave similarly, which in turn brings about a most desired condition—happiness and harmony in the bird house. Obviously it is difficult to bring the birds into breeding condition if there are discontented individuals within the group that continually disturb the nests or quarrel with the others over their places on the perches.

If an experienced bird breeder wants to keep a number of

Young zebras mature in about two months and can be sexed about three weeks after leaving the nest. Up to this time, they closely resemble females; but males will develop a few lines of the zebra throat and chest markings in the area which later will be the black concentration at the lower boundary. White zebras, of course, lack all these markings.

zebra finch pairs, he should have no trouble as long as he uses a colony breeding cage in which three or six pairs can be housed comfortably. It is extremely important to be conscientious in the management and ringing of birds to prevent undesired pairings. Otherwise you will be faced with insoluble problems after the breeding season in regard to color combinations and hereditary factors. If you have a colony breeding cage you can maintain a pure color strain. For example, if all the pure whites are kept together, you know categorically that the descendants will be white. However, bear in mind that though white zebra finches may appear to the eye to be white, they are not totally descended from pure whites! A male is not beyond stretching its "marriage vows" a bit, pairing with other females while its first mate is still in the nest brooding. As a result of all the mutations and combinations, you can well wind up the breeding season with an untold riot and variety of color. Therefore I want to give the beginner a good piece of advice: begin with only one couple so that you can later show—on paper—how the young came by their coloration. Only then can you speak of responsible breeding!

A mother zebra finch feeding her baby; notice the position of the head of the youngster! A young zebra begging for food can be heard over a long distance.

But the colony breeding cage also has its disadvantages. It is definitely undesirable if you are not certain of the hereditary background of the color. It would not be the first time that a newly purchased mutant had paired with the "wrong" bird so that nothing or almost nothing came through with the expected mutation in the next generation. If a new mutation or color appears—and that can always happen—then it makes sense to try to back-cross the "new" mutant with one of the older birds. In a colony breeding cage this is difficult to do, for who can identify with certainty the exact mother or father? However, it should be mentioned that in such a cage the most spontaneous mutations of color varieties can appear.

Zebra finches are distinctly seed-eaters. A "tropical seed mix" is prepackaged and available in all pet shops handling birds, but be sure to buy only reliable brands. After acquiring some experience you can make your own mixture, taking care to include the most important varieties of seeds. Birds have the very unmannerly habit of adding to their diet seeds they find delicious but which are not particularly healthy for them. In addition to the usual foods, grass seeds, either loose or in bundles, various millet seeds, both loose and on the spray, a little canary seed and quite a lot of half-ripe seeds should be included. Also be sure that the birds have fresh drinking water every day and water for their bath. Spread some clean river sand in a sunny corner for a sand bath, too. This promotes molting, keeps down vermin and, for some birds, is indispensable.

It is also necessary to give the birds extra morsels if you wish to keep them in top condition. They need greens such as chickweed, lettuce, chickory, endive and spinach as well as cuttlebone (available in pet shops), fresh ant eggs (actually pupae), termites and small or cut-up mealworms. This brings some variety to the daily menu. Unvaried feeding is unhealthy for all living organisms.

After the young have hatched, it is advisable to augment

the usual diet with egg-mixture and other commercial soft foods offered fresh and unspoiled each day. Old white bread soaked in water, milk or, better yet, cream can also be offered taking care that this mixture is not put in the sun where it can turn sour. Each day throw away any that is left over and make a fresh batch.

Seeds can be given individually in the feeder as well as in the mixture. In my opinion, it is better to give them separately in the feeder. If it appears that there is a shortage of a particular seed or vitamin, you can easily remedy that: just make sure that the necessary food is strewn about and the bird, with its passion for sneaking food, will eat what is required. Mixed seed has the great disadvantage of containing only a limited percentage of each type.

A pair of gray-wings or silver-wings. There is usually considerable variation in the shading of individuals, so a breeder has to work according to the standards published by the societies.

One more important point: never buy birds during a cold spell! Even if they are well packed, they can pick up sicknesses during shipping. Birds that are transported when the temperature is low must not be placed in a warm room immediately. The air in their lungs, air sacs and bones will expand too rapidly, causing extreme tension in the little body, great pain and, ultimately, death. If, due to circumstances, a bird is acquired when the weather is cold, make certain that it is given the chance to gradually accustom itself to a warmer temperature.

Whenever birds are transported by car or train, pack the shipping cage completely, leaving only a small area in the front open for air and light. If the water is used up too soon, put in some moistened bread, a wet sponge or anything else that will serve the purpose; then there is no chance that the birds will die of thirst. Of course a cup of seed should be provided. There are several things that must be attended to for all birds after being transported, even when the temperature is favorable. The continuous shaking and jerking of the cages will make the birds shy and anxious. Once they arrive at their destination the cages should be permitted to stand for about three hours so the birds have the opportunity to recover. Provide seeds and fresh drinking water, but do not take the water directly from the tap or pump—let it reach room temperature. The temperature in the wrapped cage during shipping can become quite high, and cold water can cause stomach upset and other illnesses.

It is logical to buy birds from a reliable dealer. Check to make certain the finches are vermin-free and their feathers shiny. If they seem to be picking or scratching at their feathers, you would do well not to buy them. Beaks and feet must not be covered with dirt and excrement, and the underbelly should not be messy. A bird with a soiled underbody may well be suffering from a metabolic disturbance, and it would not be advisable to buy it. Above all, buy a bird that seems unquestionably healthy, with bright, quick eyes, a

In many cases, modern aviaries consist of two adjoining parts: a wired-in or glassed-in flight and a roofed-over permanent shelter or house attached to the flight.

bird that is flying happily about the cage and not sitting sadly on its perch or sleeping with its head tucked under its wing. Also be on the look-out for birds that sit constantly in front of the feeding dish dawdling rather than eating. Check the cage itself carefully, including the drinking cups and other utensils; everything should be in the best possible order. In the greatest number of cases you will find that everything is pure and hygenic, but you cannot be too careful: an ounce of prevention is indeed worth a pound of cure.

An advantage of buying from a reliable dealer is that the birds may have been up for sale for a couple of months and have had a chance to get used to people. These birds are no longer nervous, and the novice bird owner will not have to contend with them fluttering around constantly, getting on his nerves. The truth is that most of the birds offered for sale are bred in captivity and are quite accustomed to the cage or aviary. Only a very few zebra finches are imported from their land of origin, Australia. This is regrettable since fresh new wild blood always strengthens the entire breed and prevents degeneration.

The birds demand daily attention, and anyone deciding to get involved must ask himself if he has sufficient free time to devote to their care.

How do you go about adding a new arrival to an already established group of birds? If you have read between the lines, you have surely gotten the impression that it is not easy to buy a totally healthy pair of birds. Furthermore, a newcomer will be regarded as an intruder, disturbing the harmony of the aviary. I strongly advise against adding new birds, particularly during the breeding season when the birds are housed in an outdoor aviary. In nature, each bird has its own territory, so it must also have its own domain in the cage for a sense of safety and freedom. New birds can upset the entire existing territorial arrangement. Never keep too many birds in one aviary; peace and quiet will not prevail and the chance of successful breeding will be reduced to a minimum. However, overpopulation is a problem that occurs too often. Out of necessity, if there is enough room, a few smaller cages can be built to house diverse color varieties and mutations that go well together. It is recommended that only those birds discussed later in this book be placed with zebra finches; experienced breeders can try their hand at raising more difficult varieties.

Newly purchased birds should be separated and observed for approximately two weeks to be certain they are all right. If there are still no outward symptoms of illness, you can then put them in with the others. Have the food and water ready and waiting when they first go in. After a week, add the greens, egg-food, mealworms and cod-liver oil.

It may sometimes be necessary to get one of the birds out of the breeding cage or aviary. This is easiest in an aviary, but in a brooding cage you must get the bird out by hand. Birds should be caught as seldom as possible as they become very shy. The immediate consequences of too much handling can be poor breeding or, if the catch is done clumsily, dead birds! In an aviary or colony breeding cage you can use a deep net bought in a pet shop. Wrap the wooden or metal handle with foam rubber, quilting or other soft material, otherwise you may accidentally injure one of the birds with the hard edge. The birds are best caught in the air rather than as they sit on their perches or on the wire mesh. In this way you will have the fewest mishaps. Also take care to catch only one bird at a time. If you must bring the birds in for the winter, then do not try to move them all at once, but rather do it over a period of three or more times. Otherwise they become overfatigued with distressing consequences.

Once more I want to emphasize: catch them as little as possible! If they must be handled then do so calmly and with control; rouse the birds as little as possible. In a large aviary it is advisable to make it a two-person operation; one goes into the night roost, the other shoos the birds into it and then shuts the door to the night housing. All the birds inside are

These aviaries have simplicity and trimness in design. The wooden framework and shelters are coated with a finish to enhance the grain of the wood and to blend with a rustic environment. Zebra finches and softbills live amicably in the dense underbush in these aviaries. Branches and a large clump of weed stalks provide cover and nesting sites for many varieties of finches and such. Button and harlequin quails especially like the thicket. Running water and growing shrubs add beauty to the central flight at the far end, which contains bulbuls, cardinals, thrushes, tanagers, orioles and large finches.

now caught—I am speaking only of the autumn catch when it is necessary to get all the birds out of the aviary—while the others that remain in the outer aviary during our "chase" do not need to be caught. In this way there is very little chance of accidents.

A female zebra finch feeding one of her youngsters. In the lower photo the mother is shown in the actual process of inserting food into the bill of the fledgling.

Chapter 3. Historical Background

Through qualified authorities I attempted to discover when the first zebra finches were imported into Europe, but it became quite clear to me that no definite information exists. In the beautiful *Fremdländischen Stubenvögel,* by the German ornithologist and bird expert Karl Neunzig, (issued in Maagdenburg in 1921 and reissued in 1965 by Asher and Co., Amsterdam) it appears that the zebra finches were already known in Europe as far back as 150 years ago. According to information given me by Mr. H. Rensenbrink from "Natura Artis Magistra" (Zoo "Artis") of Amsterdam, the first zebra finches, still known then under the scientific classification of *Taeniopygia castanotis,* arrived in Amsterdam in 1859. They were given the name "mandarijn amadina," which probably came from the French "diamant mandarin." "When the bird was first brought into Europe, we do not know," said Mr. Rensenbrink, "but we did find it reported that Vieillot in Paris had bred them."

Mr. R.A.Th. van Hooff, director of the Burger's Zoo, presumed that the first zebra finches were brought to London. "But when this occurred cannot be determined, since it concerned just a little insignificant bird. The zoo in Antwerp probably got one soon after London, as did "Artis," while it is probable that Berlin had one of the first. As far as I can trace back, our park received its first zebra finches in 1928; in 1929 and 1930 we bred them. Where and when the very first was bred is extremely difficult to say. Perhaps it was done by a bird enthusiast privately, or it could just as well have occurred in the animal parks of London, Berlin or Antwerp. One of the first—if not the first—importers of these finches to Holland was the firm of Blaser of Rotterdam. I don't know if the firm exists anymore. They were bird dealers, and later sold other larger animals too."

From Mr. Rensenbrink's letter in which he mentioned that zebra finches had been bred by Vieillot, I was led to the well-known book *Les Oiseaux Chanteurs* (2 vol., 1805 and 1809). Upon leafing through it, I found the notation that Vieillot had kept the finches in his aviary. One can be certain that he also bred them, for a bird so easy to care for and so quickly able to breed could have presented no difficulties for that famous bird expert.

In the 19th century over all of western Europe zebra finches became desirable and well known as breeding birds. It is interesting to note that up to the present time it is not known when the zebra finch was first bred in captivity, even in Australia. However, it was an Australian who bred the first mutation, namely the white zebra finch. If we go along with what C. af Enehjelm (Helsinki) says in his article in *Foreign Birds* (Sept. 1956), we should note the following: the

white color was bred by A.J. Woods in Sydney in an aviary in which a mixed group was housed (1921). He concerned himself with 3 young birds, which he sold to a fellow townsman named Lyons. Lyons definitely standardized the mutation and bred several hundred birds. The first white zebra finches came to Europe about 42 years ago. The silver mutation also comes from Australia; the first example reached our part of the world before the Second World War but was not as generally well known as the white, which was, often as not, grey. Unfortunately Enehjelm did not leave us any information telling precisely who bred the silver mutation nor where or when.

According to C. Stork, the first brown mutation was bred by F. Mills in South Africa (Johannesburg, 1942) while Enehjelm left open the possibility that the first brown zebra finch was of Australian origin. Enehjelm also reported that the multicolored zebra finch was bred by U. Nilsson (Copenhagen) around 1930-1935. The chestnut-flanked white zebra finch, bred by Whitehouse (Brisbane, Australia), was first observed by him in the wild and was one of the last colors to become known in Europe. When he bred them in 1937 he was only able to produce females, but many years later, as a crowning glory to his work, he succeeded in breeding a male. In 1950 the silverwing, which was originally bred in Australia, was introduced to Europe.

Opposite: The size of an aviary will have to be left to the direction of the individual fancier, but it may be mentioned that good breeding successes have been achieved in quite small aviaries. A large aviary that is overcrowded will probably give poorer breeding results than a small one with a few good pairs of birds.

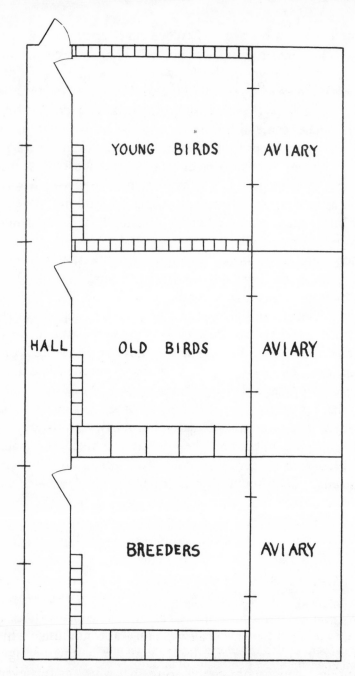

Floor plan for an outdoor aviary.

Chapter 4. Breeding in a Colony Breeding Cage or Aviary

Breeding generally occurs much more easily and spontaneously when a colony breeding cage is used rather than a cage that is only large enough for a single pair. In the colony cage the birds can choose their mates, while this is not possible in a small breeding cage. Indeed, it is possible that a couple in a single breeding cage may not get on well with each other, which could lead to poor breeding and/or poor brood care and, in general, an unsuccessful experience. Also, if it becomes necessary to remove one of the birds or put in another one of a different color, for example, complications can arise. This is not hard to understand; if a couple is attached to one another and a "stranger" suddenly comes upon the scene, a "happy marriage" can be easily upset.

If for good reason it becomes necessary to separate a well-adjusted couple, make certain that the bird which has been removed is nowhere in the vicinity of the one left behind. If this precaution is not taken—and breeders frequently make this mistake—the new couple will not learn to live together peacefully, leading to breeding failure.

We recommend the colony breeding cage as the ideal housing which permits the birds to choose their own mates. Obviously the bird keeper has no word in this choice, which presents a problem if he wishes to breed for particular color combinations. Other than that, there is the great advantage that the birds form lasting relationships, sometimes life-long.

When the couples are in an enclosed area this acts as a stimulant to intensive pairing and nest-building. This stimulation is almost totally lacking in a small single breeding cage with one couple. Birds living in a colony even in nature must work through their problems, their joys and

The main advantage of having a bird-room is that one can maintain in a temperate or cold climate many species of birds which are not sufficiently hardy in constitution to winter in outdoor aviaries. For the bird breeder, of course, a bird-room is an essential, since it offers full control. *Below:* A breeding-cage for canaries can be used for zebra finches as well.

their sorrows, and the colony breeding cage is as close as we can get to reproducing their natural environment. Breeding in a colony breeding cage sets aside whatever control you may have in fixing particular mutations, but if you are interested in breeding for a particular pure color line in one colony breeding cage, for example normal brown zebra finches, then you can achieve beautiful results.

You are not bound to the use of a colony breeding cage. If there is room enough, there are any number of different kinds of aviaries. In aviaries it is also possible to house other kinds of birds. This should cause no trouble and may be useful for several reasons. With this in mind it seemed practical to devote a separate chapter to the raising of "simple" tropical birds, although much of the information found in this book is applicable to the raising of these other birds, too.

Finally, I will repeat the following: do not try to breed too intensively. If you work with leg bands you can be sure of maintaining responsible control over the breeding without taking the chance of compounding problems. Always think about introducing "fresh blood" rather than breeding the same birds. In line with this, do not breed the young of a given pair with each other or breed their young with grandparents, nieces, nephews, sisters or brothers. Good breeders try, to the best of their ability, to breed birds that are not related to each other!

The fancier does not really know the joy of aviculture until he has bred some birds for himself. Zebra finches therefore are a good start in order to obtain young.

Chapter 5. The Breeding Season

Many breeders make the common mistake of starting breeding too early. This pertains not only to zebra finches but to all cage or aviary birds that regularly tend to mate too soon. Zebra finches should be restrained, otherwise it is possible that in the dead of winter they will be sitting on eggs in their nests and expecting the babies during the most barren season of the year. Early breeding can cause the females to lose much of their strength, which affects future broods negatively. Young birds from early matings are generally not too strong, as becomes apparent when you wish to breed them after eight months.

Begin breeding at the end of March or the beginning of April with couples that have been kept apart during the winter months. You should have kept males with males and females with females (from the bands you can see which is which). You can anticipate three to four broods that, with good care, should be striking for their purity.

Weather conditions can well be responsible for breeding success or failure. If the birds have the opportunity to rest during the winter months and build up a reserve of strength for the coming breeding season, the result will be a group of intrinsically strong, healthy offspring. I fully agree with those who contend that by this pattern of breeding you miss out on at least one round of breeding, but conversely, the new birds are of outstanding quality and the old ones do not get exhausted and can be bred successfully again the following season. Above all, use good common sense and do not begin breeding before the end of the generally wet and inclement month of March.

You would do well to keep the males and females apart except during breeding season. If you are working with a breeding cage which only accommodates one couple, then of course there is no problem about forming a definite pair. But if there is the possibility of more than one pairing, precautions should be taken. I work with a variety of small exhibition cages in which I place selected pairs for a period of about two weeks. In these cages there is barely any nest-building material and there are no nesting boxes placed at the sides. The birds can now literally "eat their bellies full," building up a fat reserve which does no harm, but they are not yet given the opportunity to breed. In this way they become accustomed to each other and, when later let loose in a colony breeding cage or aviary, they may well seek out one another and pair off for the entire breeding season. This is a good way of achieving purity of strain in descendants, if this is what you are working for. My birds have differently colored rings on their legs so I can easily keep tabs on what is happening for my written records.

There is no question that birds having a purity of particular colors—those that are *homozygous (purely descended)*—can be bred in a variety of bird houses. It is also possible that a couple brought together by the breeder might cease to exist as a couple when they come into contact with others of their own kind. Just as with people, birds prefer to make their own choice.

It is a mistake to try to prolong the breeding season by using sunlamps or other such aids. The best results are achieved by following nature. If you begin breeding at the end of March, you can continue until August. I counsel strongly against permitting egg-laying past this time because the new brood is generally weak and does not fare well. Even a short spell of bad weather can be enough to do these little ones in, not to mention the excessive exertion the female has to endure and the subsequent danger this brings about, such as the weakening of the line.

All things considered, it is not difficult to breed zebra finches as long as you stick to the general rules. Do not try to force the birds to nest if they show no inclination to do so. By having the birds you wish to breed in the vicinity of one

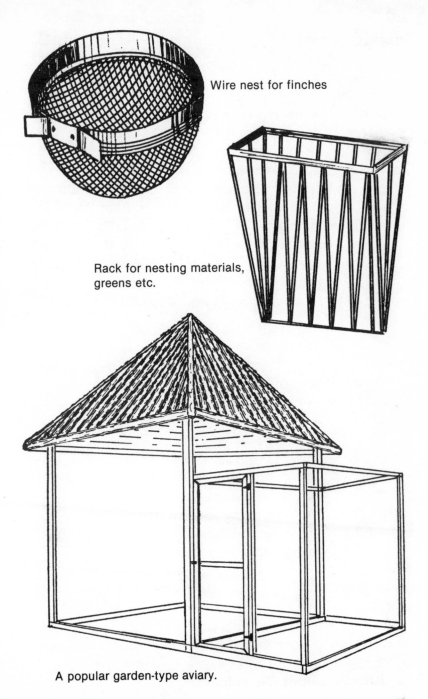

Wire nest for finches

Rack for nesting materials, greens etc.

A popular garden-type aviary.

49

another, they may well begin their nest-building. By taking these preparatory measures, the chances are that everything will proceed favorably.

It can happen that two birds absolutely do not seem suited to each other. This can be determined if you note that they keep starting to build new nests or lay an enormously large clutch of eggs which, after a few days, is covered over with a new nest. In such cases the problem is best solved by separating the birds and permitting them to pair with different mates. It goes without saying that birds from premature breeding do not make good breeding couples. I have obtained the best results with one- to four-year-olds. Birds that are too old, particularly the females, are also less well suited for breeding. It stands to reason that intrinsically healthy offspring come from intrinsically healthy parents.

Nearly all zebra finches are fond of egg-food, and in captivity this is an essential item in their diet. Because of the ease with which our seed-eating zebras are fed and managed, they are deservedly the most popular of cage and aviary birds.

It is not good to provide nest-building materials without a system. This does not mean that there should be no carpet wool, newspaper strips, hair, fibers, small pieces of cloth and such. However, too little thought is given to the nest-building materials. It is definitely not an unreasonable luxury to find good building stuff such as hay and sisal string. The zebra finch then has the opportunity to build a nest which is a strongly constructed breeding place. Do not offer the above mentioned materials all at the same time, but give the hay first and then the string. This is easy enough for cages housing only one couple but more difficult when dealing with a colony breeding cage or aviary. However, with a little forethought the nests will not be too far apart, and if they are no harm is done. If you keep strict control to make sure the building materials are kept in special racks, the birds will generally use the hay first and then work the string into the bowl of the nest.

For the most part, the construction is rather rough, just as it is in the wild. To actually construct a nest, the birds must use hay or some good substitute. The hay is used for the outside, while the interior is carefully worked with string, horsehair, wool, small feathers and the like. To avoid any unpleasant experiences, take care to pull the strands of string apart and keep them short. I cut them in lengths of 6 cm rather than run any risks. If longer threads are used you will see that they are more difficult to work in and as a result the birds flying into and out of the nest can get their feet entangled and remain hanging. Unless you are nearby to quickly rescue a bird caught in this way, it can die. This holds true for other exotic birds, particularly those that have strong claws such as the spice finch and tricolored mannikin. I already mentioned turkish carpet wool, a material I let my finches work with often; hemp fibers are good. It is interesting, and in a way rather nice, that the birds seem to prefer materials of natural color. They will use the darker colors such as red, blue or green, but to a far lesser degree.

A typical way the female zebra offers food to one of her young.

You probably know that most birds are fastidious to the point of removing the droppings of the young from the nest. After a parent has brought in the food it looks sharply at the nestling, which, needing to relieve itself, turns around a little and defecates. The parent bird takes the droppings in its bill and either hauls them away or swallows them; the latter is done by thrush-like birds. To some this may seem disgusting, but actually it is not; the droppings are neatly encased in a thin membrane.

The young always have an insatiable hunger, and their food demands are enormous. The breeder should give extra attention to the food he provides during the breeding season. Later on I will go into this subject in greater detail. Adult zebra finches—and this holds true for all kinds of birds—have tremendous appetites. They must eat a lot because they are constantly active and maintain a high body temperature. Rapid digestion is necessary to provide them with sufficient energy. Young birds eat even more. In strong and healthy growing birds, it is not uncommon for them to consume more than their own body weight within a 24-hour period! The parents are unbelievably busy keeping the supply coming.

Ornithologists have counted the number of "food flights" made by various sorts of birds. The late Dr. Arthur A. Allen of Cornell University filmed a female wren between sunrise and sunset and found that she brought in food 1217 times. The late famous Dutch biologist Dr. Jac. P. Thijsse counted 1356 flights for a blue titmouse. In the aviary I filmed the food flights of a zebra finch and counted 1237. In Queensland I did the same thing and counted, between daybreak and nightfall, 1186. Since the finding of food does not always take the same length of time, you will not get a valid picture by multiplying the number of flights made in one hour by the number of hours of daylight. You must actually count from the moment the sun comes up to the moment it disappears below the horizon.

Now the following questions may arise: do all the young get a sufficient amount of food? Isn't a single one forgotten? Does each one regularly receive his portion? The answer is always in the affirmative. When the parents come to the nest with food, all the hungry little beaks open up yawning and screaming for food, and the father or mother arbitrarily stuffs a waiting beak. If the food does not disappear quickly, it is deftly picked out again and deposited in another beak. Only the young one that swallows quickly gets the offering inside. This can be explained as follow: when food enters the nestling's throat it triggers a swallowing reflex which works more quickly and more actively in proportion to how empty the bird's craw is; the fuller the craw the slower the reflex. This works quite accurately, for you can well understand that since there are so many food flights, the offspring are almost never actually sitting with an empty craw suffering real hunger. The system is infallible.

With such frequent feedings there is naturally a large

quantity of droppings. Why one bird species is scrupulously clean in the nest and another—such as the zebra finch—far less so will always remain an open question. The zebra finch does not carry the excrement away or swallow it, but picks it out of the cup-like area of the nest and places it neatly on the rim. It is because of this practice that I urge the use of the building materials I mentioned before. They permit ventilation, so droppings quickly become hard and there is less chance of contamination.

Bird keepers who have bred zebra finches know that they are enthusiastic builders and will continue building nests until there is no more material left to build with. Therefore, it is reasonable to limit the supply of building stuff to only as much as is necessary for one round of breeding; if they are given too much they continue to build. The male handles most of the work because he takes charge of building the outside while his wife functions as architect for the interior. This keeps them so busy that they often do not get on with the business of egg-laying.

Opposite: Before the female starts to offer food the young bird tries to attract her attention (upper photo) by spreading its wings; notice the 'strange' manner the head of the juvenile bird is held. Lower photo: After the attention-getting display, the youngster is fed.

Generally speaking it is easier to breed finches in outdoor aviaries than in cages. Nevertheless, zebra finches can easily be bred in large box cages.

Chapter 6. Brooding

Brooding is a natural process, the instinctive impulse to maintain the species. When the instinct begins to manifest itself, the brooding season has started. Generally this occurs in the spring, but there are some birds that begin sooner, some later. Within the bird a process begins to take place which we can compare to a fever, but not in the sense of an illness. The temperature of the bird's body rises only in those areas where it is necessary, such as the brood spots, which are those places that are pressed against the eggs during brooding. The location of brood spots (which receive a large blood supply) can differ greatly among different varieties of birds, which should be borne in mind when comparing birds that are not related. The way of sitting on the eggs is as much determined by the shape of the nest and the location of the brood spots as by the size of the nest, the intensity of brooding and the number of eggs. If you compare brooding circumstances of a zebra finch with those of a stilt, for example, a few of these differences would immediately become apparent.

Zebra finches are recognized for their outstanding brooding qualities. Once the nest is built, the bird keeper can do little more than calmly wait. For the most part everything goes along without difficulty and there is little to worry about.

Often the nest is built in a brood-box or nesting box. Such boxes must always be placed rather high up in the aviary, not in a line but at varying heights. They should not be placed near perches and resting places because the birds might befoul each other. It is also better not to hang the nest box near feeding and drinking places. In general, zebra finches are very industrious. Most enthusiastically they will bring one brood after another to maturity. You can observe this

There are three items which make for success in zebra finch breeding. The initial stock must be of good stamina and fertility, the accomodations provided must be suitable, and the birds must be properly fed and managed.

during nest-building as the male vigorously handles the lion's share of the work. It is amusing to see how quickly building materials are accepted, and within a few minutes of its being offered a male will come by. Diligently he makes tracks to a suitable spot, often with a bundle of building stuff in his bill, and he will not rest until he has found a good place. The female is visibly calmer, as though she is quite convinced and resigned to the principal task that awaits her. She limits herself to simply shaping and placing the material brought in, although I have also observed in the aviary that the female, too, busied herself flying back and forth with building materials for the new nest. Another interesting practice was observed. The female will look for particular building materials and place them in the bill of the male, who in turn brings them to the future nursery. Such cooperation is always pleasant to see. After three or four days the nesting box is fully stuffed with the building materials and in the middle is a small, scooped out hole—the nest or brood-cup. Now the female turns her attention to the amorous behavior of her mate. As soon as she begins to move her tail rapidly up and down and back and forth, mating can occur at any moment. In the introduction a detailed description of the mating dance was given, and it need not be repeated here. A day or so after the mating (copulation) the female goes into the nest and the first egg can be expected. A complete clutch consists of three to five eggs, but later broods, of which there may be three or four per season, can have more. It is not abnormal to find a first clutch of seven eggs.

I do not advocate frequently checking the nest. The birds are very easily disturbed, with the consequence that they may abandon the eggs or, in some cases, even the young. Fortunately zebra finches are not unduly shy. I recall an instance when it was necessary to rehouse an entire nest with a complete clutch of eggs. The birds did not get out of sorts, continued to brood normally and raised a beautiful family to maturity. Checking is generally used to rectify a particular condition and, if not done too frequently, may actually be desirable. If it is necessary to interfere, it is best done after the eggs have been brooded for a week. Then you can check to see if all the eggs have been fertilized. If there are any unfertilized eggs, you should remove them. Use a small plastic spoon, not your fingers, for the shell is extremely thin. With a bit of care the eggs can be picked up without causing damage.

To determine whether or not an egg has been fertilized, you should hold it under a bright light. If the eggs have been brooded for a longer period it isn't necessary to use the light or, for that matter, to disturb the nest. The unfertilized eggs appear a distinctive muddy ashen red (I have heard it described as an "ugly" red) because of the decomposing contents. On the other hand, fertilized eggs after five days or so can be distinguished by their shiny purplish brown color due to the embryo. I look at the eggs after a week or eight days, taking them out of the nest and putting them on a kind of light box (small box with a grid and a 40 watt bulb). The grid is a net made of soft woolen threads that are not too loosely woven, otherwise the little eggs could fall through. I have also seen a hairnet used for this purpose. With a quick glance you can distinguish the fertilized eggs from the unfertilized, and against the strong light you may often see the embryo—the living creature in its earliest stages—move. Do not hold the eggs in the light too long, for the heat quickly becomes too intense and can kill the embryo. It is recommended that this process be done only once. The fact is that there is no urgent need to remove the unwanted eggs because the parents almost always work them out of the nest or cover them over in the rim of the nest. However, if you want to be certain, handle the eggs as described above.

You need not be afraid that the zebra finches will be too disturbed when you check the eggs as long as you work quickly and carefully, but bear in mind that the egg shells are extremely fragile, delicate and quite breakable. The smallest scratch is fatal and the egg will become worthless. Beginning breeders would be well advised to practice handling unfertilized eggs first. The egg check should be done by the person who cares for the birds all the time. It can be understood that when the birds are accustomed to a particular handler they will not be so alarmed when the nest is tampered with.

In captivity zebra finches brood for 12 to 14 days or sometimes a half or full day longer depending on weather conditions, even in an aviary. The babies are usually not hatched all at the same time, but when they leave the nest there will be no apparent size difference among the offspring; they all fly out of the nest within 24 to 28 hours of each other.

Newly received birds should be immediately turned into a cage, even if received late at night, when a good light should be left on near the cage until morning. Water is the first thing they should be given, and then some seed and perhaps a few mealworms or such. Birds newly purchased should not be put into an aviary straight away, unless you know they have come from a similar habitation and are perfectly healthy and fit. Most fanciers have a quarantine cage into which all newly bought birds are put for a few days. This is a wise safeguard against introducing infectious diseases among your stock. (By the way: these cages are ideal for breeding purposes!)

Research has shown that the last bird hatched is fed intensively for at least three or four days, which would account for the fact that it quickly becomes identical to its older siblings.

With the egg tooth—a little horny "knob" on the point of the upper beak—the young work their way through the shell and then lie naked, helpless, panting and exhausted on the bottom of the nest bowl. The little bit of down with which they are covered dries out quickly. As soon as the nestlings are a bit rested, they immediately begin to beg for food. After a day or so the egg tooth falls off, for it no longer serves any purpose. After one week you can generally make out which color variety you have, as the primary feathers begin to show.

All breeders agree that newly hatched zebra finches are quite weak, yet they are the strongest of all the tropical and sub-tropical birds. This is due to the fact that they have been kept in cages and aviaries for so long that they have become completely adapted to captivity and climate.

In the wild as well as in captivity it can happen that a parent leaves the nest too suddenly and by accident a nestling remains hanging onto one of their feet. The little bird tumbles to the ground or the floor of the aviary, but if you come quickly upon the scene and put the baby back in the nest, you will be surprised how rapidly it recovers. To avoid such accidents, try to disturb the birds as little as possible during the brooding season. When you are filling the feeding dishes or freshening their water supply, do so with calm and controlled movements. Never make a lot of motions or talk with anyone watching on the outside. Indeed, if you must enter the aviary, visitors must keep their curiosity under control and stay away from the immediate vicinity of the wire screening. The birds become disquieted whenever anyone enters the aviary, so there is little point in alarming them unnecessarily. If possible, have onlookers keep a good distance.

Let us go back now to discussing the nestlings. Very soon their craws are stuffed full of food pre-softened by the parents. Tiny pieces of the broken egg shells are eaten by the older birds, and the larger pieces are worked into the rim of the nest so that any evidence of the recent hatch is removed instinctively to protect the young from enemies. This is done by all birds, even in captivity.

When the offspring are about a week old, you can clearly hear the "food call." Each bird is fed in the manner described earlier. In the darkness of the nesting bowl it could be rather difficult for the parents to see exactly where they should put the food, but nature has provided a beautiful solution: on either side of the black beak (which actually at the very beginning is horn-colored) are small luminous spots, and two more can also be found on the very tip of the tongue. Moreover, these luminous papillae or pimple-like projections can be found on the inside of the beaks and by the throat cavity. It would get too involved to discuss these papillae further, but it is worth noting that ornithologists have come across other papillae that differ in color, intensity and location. The papillae also serve the additional function of stimulating the parents to bring in food.

It may happen that one of the young birds flutters out of the nest a few days too soon in order to get away from the crowded little bowl in which anywhere from four to seven birds may be squeezed. If it is a good summer, the little bird can be left on the aviary floor, where he will get all the food he needs. If it really is still too small and too sparsely feathered, then it would be better to return it to the nest. When you do this, patiently hold your hand in front of the nest opening until all the birds inside are calm. Also return the bird to the nest if rain or wind is expected. It is quite possible that the same bird will spend the night in the nest but the next morning seek his freedom again. In this case, do not try to put it back. Such birds are restless and tend to stir the other offspring into leaving the nest, which can be most undesirable.

The general rule is that the birds can leave the nest when

Young zebra finches still have black bills; the proud father sits on the right.

they are fully feathered, usually after 18 to 22 days. At this point they will also let themselves be given food in their beaks. It is a charming sight to see the little zebra finches begging. They flap impatiently with their wings, which practically drag on the ground, and turn their heads in a distinctive way. If the mother or father does not give them immediate attention, the cry for food becomes stronger, more urgent and more penetrating. It is not unusual for it to be heard dozens of meters away. After another week or two, the young ones can begin to care for themselves a bit, but they often continue to beg for food. They don't beg only from their own parents, but also from other zebra finches which are caring for their broods. Indeed, when these others become overburdened by the supplications of the young birds, peculiarly enough, the whole bird community in the aviary helps the "little beggars" to grow up and become self-sufficient. Just because they have become self-reliant

Above: side and front views of two male wild color, gray or normal zebra finches. *Below:* two male cinnamons (back and front); inset: yellow-billed female cinnamon.

Indoor breeding cages are designed primarily for canaries, but zebra finches can be housed in these cages as well and will bring up brood after brood if one takes care of the birds.

definitely does not mean that they should be permitted to breed yet. Not only have they just come into full color, but their internal organs are not fully matured. This applies particularly to the females. They should all be provided with leg bands and placed in different cages or aviaries, separated by sex. When the birds are between eight months and a year old they can be considered sexually mature and can be used for breeding.

After August, breeding should be completely stopped. It is true that one more brood can be brought to maturity in September, but before the young birds are really independent it is already October, and this—in general—is not a particularly summer-like month. The young from late broods are often "misfits." They will never be good birds to exhibit and as brooders for the next season they are worthless. The fancier may well be stuck with unfertilized eggs, abandoned nests and other undesirable occurrences. At the end of August you would do better to involve yourself with preparations for the autumn cleaning of the aviary and in taking inventory. More importantly, the separated males and females can look forward to a well earned rest after a busy breeding season and you can look forward to the following year with the expectation of four broods per couple.

Above: two females of the wild color (inset, back and front). *Below:* female cinnamons (back and front).

Above: two silver males (back and front); inset: dark-cheeked silver male. *Below:* two cream males (back and front).

Zebra finches are extremely interesting birds with sometimes a curious behavior during the breeding season.

Chapter 7. Curious Behavior Patterns During Brooding

From time to time the male zebra finch starts building at fever pitch a sleeping nest for his young. Such sudden, strange behavior of one or sometimes both parents is not abnormal, but is rather a spontaneous reaction to some inner need that is hard to define. Very often there are real circumstances that cause some particularly unusual behavior that cannot be explained by instinct but rather is simply the result of the fact that the bird keeper, or in some cases nature itself, has by neglect or oversight left something undone. Then the bird, in response to his impulse to maintain the species (through the breeding process), must seek other ways that seem to us strange and inexplicable.

First I will discuss *"apartment building"* or "nest over nest" situations that are not infrequent in large aviaries with a sizable population. There are several important causes that can lead to the building of such structures. The first cause involves the "guilty" female. Sometimes the female, after laying two or three eggs, has physiological difficulties that prevent her laying a full clutch. The immediate result is that the male is activated, often with surprisingly intensive assistance from the female, to build a new nest on top of the first one. The first eggs laid are of course totally lost. Difficulties can occur a second and third time so that again and again the original nest is covered over by a new one. In the wild it seems that the same thing occurs, but generally for different reasons. In Queensland I found that immediately after the sudden arrival of a severe drought all 23 nests of a small colony were covered over with new nesting material. When I later returned to the same spot, it appeared that 19 nests were abandoned while the remaining four contained new eggs. The other birds had preferred to build new nests.

Above: back and front views of two silver females. *Below:* two cream females (back and front).

Above: two penguin gray males (back and front). *Below:* two penguin cinnamon males (side and front).

In the wild the nest usually is flask-shaped, but in captivity the birds seldom build their own nests (except sometimes in an outdoor aviary). In all cases that have come under the author's observations the nest has always been spherical, with the entrance in front. These photos show a partially completed nest and the start of 'apartment building' on top of the carton nest box.

In the aviary "apartment building" can occur with healthy but older pairs, perhaps 14 months old.

"Apartment building" can also happen when there is an overabundance of nest-building material. The birds are activated to such an extent that they will completely shut off the first nest, often containing a complete clutch of eggs, and build a second right on top of it. In this case it is almost always the male that busies himself with this task, the female far less commonly being involved. In the wild this phenomenon seldom occurs. The old nests are quite transparent and made of very little building material.

A third cause for "apartment building" can be the mismatching of a pair that did not mate spontaneously but were brought together by the breeder after either the male or female had originally paired with a different bird. If the first mate of the female is visible or within hearing distance, "apartment building" could begin immediately. Whenever there is a situation that requires a contented pair to be separated, be sure that the bird removed is placed in a totally different area. It makes good sense not to separate couples before the breeding season is over, and in the middle of brooding it is best to leave the birds alone. Otherwise you can only create unrest among birds that would otherwise breed well. The only other way of dealing with separating the birds is to use separate brood cages—one cage per couple. Then, with no difficulty, one of the birds can be removed and another put in its place. If the birds are given enough time to get to know each other, it is by no means out of the question that a new pair will be formed and have at least one or more broods in the current season. The bird that had been taken out can be coupled with another partner, and in many cases the new pair get on without difficulty. If nothing comes of this pairing, then you must assume that the particular bird is unsuited for further breeding and should not be worked with anymore.

"Apartment building" can also occur when nesting boxes

Above: two penguin gray females (back and front). *Below:* two penguin cinnamon females (back and front).

Above: two frosted gray males (back and front). *Below:* two blackbreast gray females (back and front).

Napoleon weaver. This West African weaver closely resembles the orange weaver, although it is easier to breed depending on space and food provided. It will fare better in a roomy aviary than in a cage, and once acclimated can even winter in an outside flight as long as there is enough protection from north and east and a covered shelter is available.

are too big, these nests becoming filled to the very opening with stored material. Even in the open air in an outside aviary, where just about the best results are achieved (I have always had better luck with outside aviaries than with those in the house), apartment building can occur when the nest boxes are too deep. A word of good advice: do not set up deep nesting boxes, although deep models can be filled with nest-building material to within 4 cm under the exit hole, which lessens the problem somewhat.

There is very little difference between the sleeping nest and the brood-nest; it is usually just more sloppily made. You can imagine that the sleeping nests in the aviary are a far cry from the brood-nests we encounter in the wild in Australia.

The male has a funny way of making sure that his offspring disappear into a sleeping nest at night: he often has something enticing in his beak to lure the young ones to bed. More sleeping nests should be built if needed. In Queensland I have observed males in the evening with termites in their beaks, directing the young ones into different nests. As far as I could tell, the fathers were not particularly concerned whether it was just their own brood or some others that they bundled off to sleep. One zebra finch, for example, brought 12 young to different nests, although he himself was the father of just four! During beautiful summer weather with hot days, aviary males may not direct the little ones to sleeping nests, but rather to a protected spot or strong branch in the aviary. In the wild, however, sleeping nests are always used. When the male has chosen a suitable spot, you must be very sure no cats can get near it. For this reason double screening is highly recommended.

Above: normal (wild) male, frontal view of young male blackbreast.
Below: adult male blackbreast (back and front).

Above: two white females (back and front). *Below:* two white males (front and side).

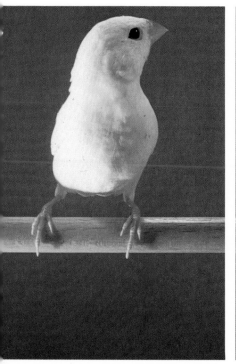

Try always to breed zebras with the same heredity pattern; only by selection this is possible.

Chapter 8. Champion Birds Through Painstaking Selection

If you happen to wander around an exhibition, you will find that birds are not classified by color alone but by their form and condition as well. A breeder who is sloppy in his work will not get very far. His dreams of "prize money" will never materialize, and his birds will degenerate into pathetic little feathered lumps. The breeder whose main objective is to breed as many birds as possible regardless of color, form or condition will discover that after he reaches his objective his birds will be nothing but unsuitable material that even the inexperienced beginner will shy away from. The man who really has his heart in his work will not rest before he can breed *choice* birds. He can rightly ask a fair price for his *breeding* birds, and only he may call his birds that because he knows what he is talking about.

How does one arrive at that point? Not surprisingly, the best guarantee of good birds is the rigorously carried through yearly selection process. Throughout this book the greatest emphasis has already been placed upon the importance of having good, prime condition couples. Those that are sick and need to be given all sorts of medication may recover but will not be of first quality color, condition and form. Such birds are good for keepers who are only interested in raising birds as a sort of sport or hobby but have no intention of exhibiting or breeding for profit. It is best to spend the first few years breeding birds for fine condition and then concentrate on color.

The second possibility for you to try, once you have healthy quality birds, is to breed zebra finches with precisely the same heredity pattern that the breeder has worked out. You cannot do this until you have worked out your own routine. This routine is completely relative, in view of the

Above: two cinnamon blackbreast females (back and front). *Below:* two cinnamon blackbreast females (back and front).

Above: two cinnamon blackbreast males (back and front). *Below:* one cinnamon zebra finch female and a white society finch.

The bicheno finch, also called white-rumped bicheno, is a friendly but delicate bird.

A pair of zebra finches on top of their nest.

fact that an old experienced hand at the business of bird breeding has to struggle with the same difficulties as the beginner; namely, you want to determine which hereditary factors went into producing those good healthy birds. The question of luck plays a big part in this because it does not generally happen that you can get your hands on a purely descended (homozygous) couple. When you think you have finally gotten such a couple, after several broods you may look in the nest and suddenly discover that there are babies in there with strange colors that were never observed either in the mother or father. If you have impurely (heterozygous) descended zebra finches, this can be remedied and is certainly no reason to give up bird keeping.

To get the most purely bred zebra finches possible, you may work with only one color or with more than one color as long as each is kept completely separated from the others in a cage or aviary, for example, grey with grey, white with white, cream with cream or fawn-brown with fawn-brown. If you immediately start breeding colors with mutations, you will get a variegated collection of colors and miscolors and have nothing to start with.

Very often the breeder cannot tell from the outward appearance of a bird whether he has a completely pure (homozygous) color or mutation in his aviary or cage. The birds may not possess any observable identifying marks (they are said to be *split* for such a marking), which may well become visible later in the next offspring. He must therefore keep on top of the situation. When he knows that his white zebra finches breed pure white, then it is simple to follow the rules of heredity we have learned—that the crossing of a white with a white will give a pure white. By ringing particular colors you can easily distinguish the offspring from other birds. You can understand how important this is if you wish to breed further. It is also an exacting science to achieve success in the breeding of other color variations and mutations.

It was mentioned earlier that grey (pure grey) sometimes

A male normal penguin (top), male fawn (center) and recessive silver female (lower).

A pair of penguin zebra finches: the male is on top the female below.

A pair of zebra finches roosing close together.

Three munias: on the right the well-known spice finch from India; the two birds on the left are the seldom imported, smaller, and less colorful spotted munia from the Philippines.

becomes inbred. When you are sure that you have a pure-grey zebra finch and you want to breed it with another color, there is no cause for concern. The new issue will be just as described in this book. On the other hand, if you have *impurely* bred grey zebra finches, you may get later generations with colors that do not belong at all with the expected color or mutation.

In order to get a pure breeding stock, you must keep the birds separated by color. The impure offspring that can appear from various crossings (such as white young with grey in their feathers) are then removed. In the long run this is how you get a homozygous white breeding stock. Naturally the parents are removed because, as seen from their offspring, they are not pure-bred. With this process you develop a strain that is pure white genetically and externally. Needless to say, this does not happen in short order and certainly not if you first have to seek out the homozygous birds from all the birds you have. Those of pure white descent may be among the younger as well as the older birds. You can avoid these difficultes if you buy homozygous individuals from a reliable breeder. There is no doubt that it can be very interesting to try to build up your own stock with identical heredity factors, even if it does take a long time. You will probably have to pay a breeder a bit more, but later on you can ask a fine price for your own pure-bred offspring. Be thoroughly aware that such birds are not to be exploited. Use them sparingly and leave the experimenting to those who raise birds only for profit.

Above: two white males (back and front). *Below:* two isabel males (back and front).

Above: two dominant silver females (back and side). Below: two isabel females (back and front).

With certain birds, especially immature birds, pairs can only be selected with some amount of luck; practically all varieties of zebra finches, however, don't present this problem, as the males are easily determined by their black marking on the chest. Keep in mind that only healthy parents produce healthy young!

Chapter 9. Special Attention for the Young Zebra Finch

To tell the young zebra finches apart, they must be ringed, a nerve-wracking and miserable job, particularly for those who have never done it before. If you keep calm, all will go well. Rings punched with the date and reference number are often provided by associations but are also available in bird supply shops. When you keep a record, you can never forget the information. Birds from the 1979 breeding season, for example, get a ring with that date; the reference number makes it possible to tell from which parents the offspring come (for example, 5, 6 and 7 come from parents 1978, ref. no. 2 and 3).

How do you ring a zebra finch? Take the bird loosely in the right hand so that one of the feet can be easily held with the thumb and forefinger. With your left hand smear the claw with petroleum jelly; the longest three toes are placed on top of each other and brought forward while the shortest toe lies in the back and is stuck to the leg by the jelly. Everything is now lying in a line so that the ring can be easily slipped on. This should be done when the birds are seven or eight days old.

For ringing older birds, it is best to use a clamp ring, a sort of clip that can be pinched closed with your nails or fingertips. You must be extremely careful, for the young bird's leg is quite tender and can be easily broken or damaged. There are also colored rings that are used on older birds when there is some uncertainty as to when they were hatched. These color rings are made of light metal or plastic and are often spiral-shaped. The metal color rings are generally of the clamp type. They are used when there is no other way of recognizing and identifying the bird. When you have, for example, one pair of fawn-brown zebra finches that have not

Above: two dominant silver males (front and back). *Below:* two variegated gray females (back and front).

The black-cheeked waxbills are insectivorous and are quite delicate until acclimated.

been ringed, it is not necessary to put the colored ring on them; their young can be ringed in the usual way with the normal closed ring.

Color rings are often handy when you have different birds of one and the same color together in a cage or aviary: couple A gets a green ring, B a yellow, C a red, etc. This saves a lot of searching. It might happen that in a very busy breeding season the bird keeper forgets to ring the young birds. If he knows after they have flown out of the nest which are their parents, nothing is lost. Many times I have seen bird fanciers in such a situation "decorate" their birds with the normal closed rings, which is indeed troublesome, but possible. There is really no point in putting closed rings on young birds out of the nest when you are not sure of the parents. This can easily happen in large groups living together in an aviary when all the different couples are of the same color.

Left: Even a small cage and a nest box may be sufficient for a pair of zebras to rear a family . . . but there are better ways! *Below:* A canary breeding cage, also usable for breeding zebra finches.

Right: We still have a lot to discover about the exact food requirements of birds in captivity, but it has been found that a more varied diet is necessary for maintaining birds in health and condition than was formerly thought adequate. *Below:* A small collection of finches can easily and happily be housed in a standard flight cage which is at least double the size of a standard canary cage.

As I said, ringing is best done when the birds are seven or eight days old. There is one difficulty which arises as a result of the ring: the parents try to get the little shiny contraption out of the nest and it doesn't seem to bother them that a little bird is attached to it! What can we do? Over the years there has been a wealth of advice published, but the method used by Mr. J. Meerburg seems to me to be the best. In an article in *De Vogelgids* (July 1966, vol. 11, no. 127) he told of his own experience with Indian silverbills and African silverbills, but this method is applicable to zebra finches, too. With permission from the publisher I cite a portion of his article.

"My couple, consisting of an African silverbill male and an Indian silverbill female (the best combination), began to nest in February. I had purposely chosen this combination because I had a number of eggs from the Indian silverbill female and the regular brood from the African silverbill, and I wanted to see them brought together in one nest. In spite of the availability of much larger nesting sites, they chose to build their nest in a coconut shell that was barely as big as a fist and which I had hung up simply as a decoration. The first time around, they hit the bull's-eye. The clutch consisted of seven eggs, all of which developed to maturity. The parents began brooding with the second or third egg (all the eggs do not necessarily hatch at the same time), but this causes no difficulty because the parents continue to feed the birds that have flown out of the nest as well as those that remain.

"When the young ones were about three weeks old, they left the nest in which they had undoubtedly been packed like sardines in a can. Within a few weeks they started building another nest in exactly the same coconut after I had cleaned it out. This time there were eight eggs, all of which developed. I was somewhat late with the ringing (I had not ringed the first brood at all),

African silverbill. Though soberly colored, this is a particularly charming little bird and a great favorite with all fanciers. It is a small bird, and the cock has a habit of warbling faintly at frequent intervals.

101

but after I greased their little legs with tallow, I was fortunate in being able to ring all eight including the two oldest offspring. When I checked the nest the next time, all the rings were neatly in place. Everything seemed fine and the birds were about to start flying out. When the first two young birds flew out, it struck me that both of them, contrary to one unringed offspring from the first nest, sat peacefully in a corner on the ground. They looked healthy enough but they did not fly. 'They will get around to it soon,' I thought to myself. I thought the same thing when four more left the nest together and joined the other two sitting in the corner. They also looked quite good and fed regularly, so why should I feel concerned? Only when all except the last had flown out, did I discover the drama that was playing itself out. This last one also joined the other six and then I knew something had to be wrong. When I decided to catch it—causing all the others who had been sitting calmly to go scooting off in all directions—I discovered to my dismay that the ringed leg was broken. My first impulse was to take this poor creature who was maimed through my doing and thrust him to the ground, thus ending his suffering. But when I saw those lively little eyes looking at me I tried to repair the damage I had caused by the late ringing. With half a split matchstick shoved under the ring I had a splint for the leg and secured it with two strips of transparent adhesive tape. I also splinted the other leg with the shaft of a chicken feather split lengthwise. Just as I was going to put the bird back in the nest, I was suddenly struck with the terrible suspicion—could the same thing be wrong with the others, too? Indeed, it was. All the little ones had one or two broken legs. It happened because the parents had tried to remove the rings. I was furious with myself. All of this had been caused by my stupidity! I am giving all those who are against our lovely hobby of bird keeping a chance to call me an animal abuser and a brute. My answer is that I would be an abuser of animals if I had, out of shame, kept silent about this dreadful experience. Theoretically, I would agree with them, considering the suffering it caused the birds. It is my purpose to write about this dreadful experience in as much detail as possible in order to help prevent the same thing from happening to you. Before I go further, I want to tell you that all eight birds fully recovered and were able to use their legs normally. Give the parents a chance to get used to the rings. I have seen a variety of African silverbills and Indian silverbills ringed where absolutely nothing went wrong, which proves that it is definitely possible. But I tried to find a

Indian silverbill. This bird has a white rump (the African silverbill has a black one); the tail is blackish and rather long and pointed. The cock is slightly purer white on the breast than the hen and a bit richer in color tone.

Bengalese (society) finches breed better in a cage than in an aviary. Unfortunately, the sexes are alike, and cocks can only be determined when they are seen displaying to the hens.

method of ringing that on the one hand would be completely safe and on the other hand would be acceptable in every respect to the birds as well as the keeper. I came up with this: when the offspring were six days old I put on a closed leg ring. When they are so young it is easy to slide the ring on. This also means that if the parents want to remove it, it will come off without injury to the baby's leg. Indeed, when I checked the next day, the parents had gone to the trouble of removing every single ring. Again I replaced the rings and again they were removed. Toward the end, I ringed the birds before I went to work and again in the evening when I came home. On the third day I noticed that a couple of the babies still had their rings on. After I had ringed the others any number of times, I caught the parents and put brightly colored clip rings on them (they had not been ringed before). I hoped to direct the attention of the parents away from the young birds by distracting them with rings of their own. My strategy worked beautifully. The older birds were so preoccupied with their rings that they completely forgot about the off-spring. Moreover, they had become somewhat accustomed to all of the rings. Right after the young could fly out, I removed the clip rings from the adults. Now that the offspring could fly surely and quickly, the parents no longer concerned themselves with the rings on the little legs."

So much for the article. I want to close this section with one last observation: ring the birds while they are still lying in the nest. After the ringing, clean the leg and toes well with a wad of absorbent cotton. Keep an eye on the parents when you put the baby back in the nest, and check the young birds when they first fly out of the nest to see if any of their legs are broken. Perhaps it makes good sense to check the birds a couple of days after you have ringed them, too. Black rings can also be used, but you must be certain that the paint contains no harmful ingredients; bird dealers can provide you with this information. With black rings there is a somewhat smaller chance that the attention of the parents will be attracted.

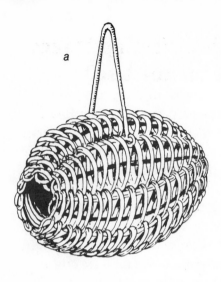

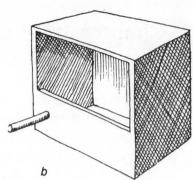

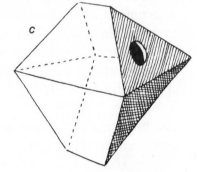

a. Finch nest
b. & c. Nesting boxes
d. Basket nest
e. Wire finch nest

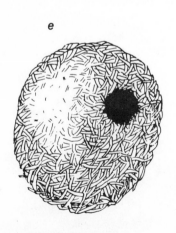

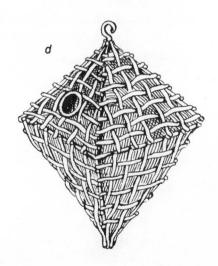

Chapter 10. Which Nesting Boxes Do Zebra Finches Use?

As I remarked before, zebra finches are not terribly discriminating when it comes to choosing good nesting material or exactly the right nesting box. They are "half-hole brooders," which refers to birds that make use of half-opened nesting boxes. This does not mean that they ignore other possibilities. I have seen one couple in one season make use of three different kinds of nests. The first was half a coconut (open), the second a whole coconut (hole brooder), and the third a half-opened nesting box (half-hole brooder). You can see that you may be in for a number of surprises during the breeding season. Just be sure that you always give the birds plenty of choice.

Actually, I believe that zebra finches prefer to move into a half-open nest box, or less often, a closed one. However, they may well go off and build their own nest completely in a bush or hedge. Bird keepers who wish to give their birds as much opportunity as possible to breed in the most natural way may consider such a free-nest style. If you feel that free-nest building may be desirable, I would not turn you against it but would point out that it is difficult to check on such nests. In each case you must bring little bundles of heather to the hedges or bushes. The birds will gratefully make use of it and build a rough but adequate nest.

There are many types of nest boxes that can be purchased, but if you are at all handy you can easily make them yourself. Those who breed their birds in aviaries without a roof must make the nests wind- and rain-proof. The boxes can be covered with tar paper. Never forget to put ventilation holes in the boxes. This is extremely necessary because of the quantity of droppings. Boxes without ventilation quickly become terribly stuffy, particularly on hot days. As a result, the young have a tendency to want to leave the nest several days too soon, and they never use it as a sleeping place. Hang the nest boxes as much in the shade as possible. Never make nest boxes out of plywood, because dampness can make the layers of wood become unglued and form a breeding place for vermin. Earwigs find good hiding places there too. Worse yet, the loose pieces of wood can be a breeding place for lice and bacteria. Such vermin can wreak havoc among young birds! Nest boxes are preferably made from beech, oak or any hard wood that has been well seasoned. Boxes made from other kinds of materials last for only one breeding season, but those made of wood can stay in good condition for years. Of course, the nest boxes should be removed after each brooding season and thoroughly cleaned. Every pet shop catering to birds has excellent products made for cleaning the boxes and perches.

Zebra finches, like all aviary birds, like to sleep high up, so hang perches and nesting boxes as high as possible. Do not put the nests too close to each other; they should be at least 50 cm apart to keep the birds from squabbling. In nature each bird has his own territory where he is master, and this is true in the cage and aviary, too.

Finally, remember that you must provide a far greater number of possible brooding places than you have couples. At least two to three times the number of nest boxes as there are pairs of birds is your best bet.

An attractive aviary designed for housing foreign finches and/or canaries.

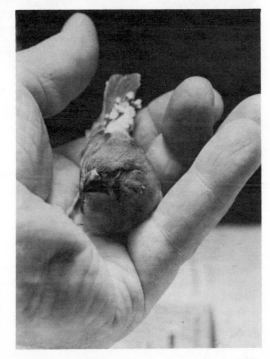

A young zebra finch just out of the nest.

Breeding zebra finches presents no problems. They are easy to house in aviaries and large cages. The species is quite domesticated and comes in a variety of colors. The zebra therefore is the ideal bird for the beginner in the keeping and breeding of foreign birds. They even make excellent foster parents.

Chapter 11. Perches and Sleeping Places

Two kinds of sticks are used as perches. The most commonly used perches are round and not too thin; the top side is somewhat flattened. You must make a distinction between *swinging* perches and *stationary* perches, both of which should be made of hardwood. The swinging ones can be thought of as play perches, while the stationary ones are absolutely essential during copulation. Thinner sticks used by the birds are generally found on the natural plants that may be around and are used solely for playing. However, if they are well formed and set up properly, they may make good nesting places. During the summer months the birds use the perches as sleeping places as well, but it is a good idea to have separate sleeping areas for them, too. In an inside aviary or in the roofed-over area of an outside aviary, it will suffice to have stationary, round, not too thin perches of hardwood. In the outside aviary, the sleeping houses should be hung in wind- and draft-free places with one side completely open. They should be of hardwood with the bark removed so they will stay free of lice and can be easily cleaned. The perches must not be so thin that the toes of the birds can close completely around them and thus keep the birds from resting comfortably. A thicker perch also keeps the nails from growing too long. However, the perches should vary a bit in thickness to help keep the muscles of the legs supple.

Because the birds like to sleep high up, the roosting perches must also be placed high. Make sure that there is sufficient room between roosts to avoid arguments, and take particular care that one stick is not directly above the other, otherwise the birds on top will befoul those below. If you are using a colony breeding cage for your zebra finches, the

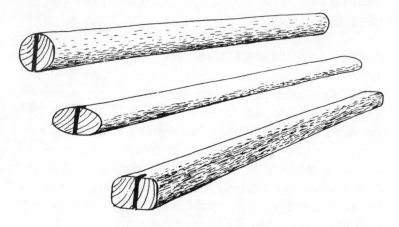

Manufactured perches

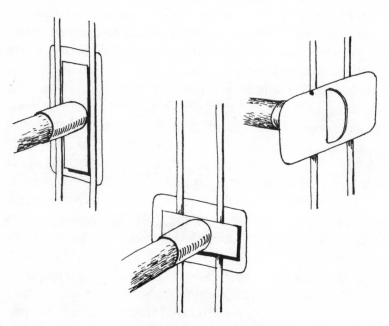

Twist grip for perch ends

same precautions of course apply. Carefully place the perches in such a way that the birds are not hindered in their flight. Perches should not be put into the breeding cage before the nesting places are set up; this prevents "undesired visitors" from having the oppportunity to look into places where they have no business. Always try to prevent arguments among the birds, particularly among those that are breeding.

It is very nice to have a cage equipped with little swings, see-saws, wheels, etc., but in breeding cages and aviaries it is fundamentally wrong. These toys are good for parrakeet-like birds, but for "tropical birds" (which includes the zebra finch) they are taboo.

Perches made of artificial materials should be designed and placed in such a way that they can easily be removed without disturbing the birds too much.

Perhaps it is unnecessary to say that in winter sleeping places must be provided, but be sure to take away all nesting materials if you do not keep your birds apart. However, it really does make good sense to separate the males and females as the winter sets in.

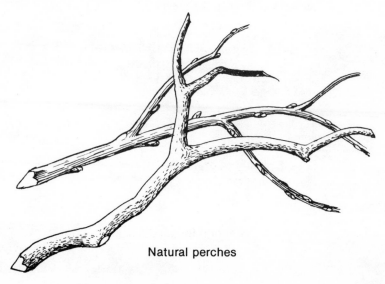

Natural perches

Seed germination requires any birdseed (millet, whiteseed) which is fresh. You need an aluminum tray, a strainer, bowl and plastic wrap. The strainer must fit into the bowl (1) and be able to support itself on the rim. Fill the strainer with the seed and rinse it under running water until it is thoroughly clean. Allow it to soak for 24 hours in the bowl. Change the water as frequently as convenient, but at least once every 12 hours. Then pour the dampened seed onto the tray (2) and spread the seed uniformly. (3) Mix in any mold-inhibiting substance (Moldex) and cover the seed to keep the moisture in, but not to stop air from getting to the seed (4).

Chapter 12. Food and Drinking Water

There are many hygenically packed brands of seeds in the store. Several of them have world-wide reputations, and rightly so. The different kinds of seeds found in the shop are well known nutritionally and have been tested in laboratories. The mixed tropical seeds which are important for our birds can be used with confidence. For breeders who prefer to get their seeds separately—and there is much to be said for this—I will give here the most important seeds that zebra finches and other tropical birds mentioned in this book should be given:

yellow millet (called La Plata)	4 parts
Senegal millet	4 parts
white millet	2 parts
white (canary) seed	2 parts
broken hemp	1 part

For those who wish to give this seed mixture, always use the best quality seeds and mix in the proportions given, namely 4:4:2:2:1. During the winter months the percentage of hemp seed can be increased a bit. As an extra tidbit twice a week, you can surprise the birds with germinated grass seed (either grown by you or bought in a shop). In addition, there should be a daily serving of greens in the form of lettuce, chickweed, Belgian endive, chicory or germinating plants like millet. I cannot warn too strongly against serving greens that have been sprayed with disinfectants and insecticides. These can be deadly. Even cooking or washing them yourself does not guarantee 100% safety.

It would be ideal if every bird keeper had a little garden of his own where he could grow greens, but this is not always possible, so we are dependent upon the greens from the market. The least we can do is wash everything thoroughly

Left: Millet spray is relished by all zebra finches as a treat food. *Below:* Cuttlebone is necessary, as it provides calcium. The soft side should be accessible to the birds.

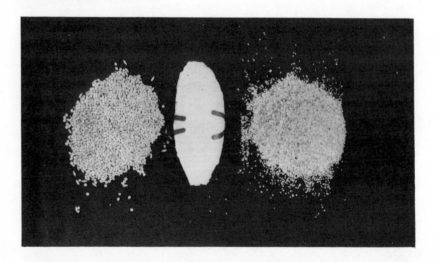

under running water and shake off as much moisture as possible. It is safer not to give the birds wet greens, as this is a source of sickness. It is also preferable to give the inner leaves from lettuce or chicory. Put the greens in racks rather

116

than placing them on the floor or ground of the cage or aviary, a practice that is far from hygenic and also very unsightly. Every bird enclosure should have a container of broken oyster shells or shell sand with finely crushed charcoal mixed in. A cuttlebone or ground egg shells should also be placed in the cage.

To aid molting as well as egg-laying, during the last weeks of the breeding season and with the coming of autumn it is a good idea to mix a bit of codliver oil into the seeds. Do not "drown" the seeds in the oil; just add two or three drops to one kilo (2.2 pounds) of seed. In the winter months this ration can be doubled. Remember that too much oil can cause diarrhea or constipation.

The menu is not yet complete. Every day, in winter as well as summer, the birds should have a slice of old white bread soaked in milk or water. Any that is left over from the previous day should, of course, be thrown away to prevent sickness. On very warm days the soaked bread should be placed out of the sun and not allowed to remain in the cage for more than three hours in order to avoid spoilage. In the breeding season fresh ant eggs, cut-up mealworms and small whiteworms should be included in the diet. Italian millet should also be included. All tropical and subtropical birds love it, and zebra finches are no exception.

When automatic feeders are used for seeds, the chance of the food getting fouled is practically impossible. The seed husks should then be removed every day by just blowing them, which takes very little time.

Finally, soft foods and commercial egg-foods of the best quality should be given. This is served in porcelain dishes, glazed pottery, galvanized iron chicken feeders or the like. Do not give too much of this food, as it is subject to spoilage. The feeders must never be hung in the open section of an outdoor aviary. All the instructions for serving the foods mentioned and the conditions for feeding hold good for all tropical birds.

Female zebra finch preparing to feed one of her hungry youngsters.
The highly ritualized behavior of the fledgling zebra finch is not
found among most of the other Australian grassfinches.

Water

The ideal method of providing drinking water is to have a small rocky mound with rivulets of running water. Putting in such a system is expensive, and it must be turned off in the winter. Therefore, most bird keepers make do with earthenware bowls. Actually this is not very hygenic because the birds also like to bathe in the same bowl and dirt and dust can get in. Little fountains and automatic drinking containers suffer from the same problem but to a far lesser degree since they refill themselves and, for the most part, it is difficult for the birds to take a bath in them. You could also cover the drinking bowls with wire mesh. In the winter, ice serves this same purpose. It is quite possible that birds bathing in the winter can die from freezing, so you should check every two days during the winter that everything is under control. In the summer, check every day. The bath water should be refilled several times a day because the bowls quickly become dirty. This is a regular and necessary daily chore.

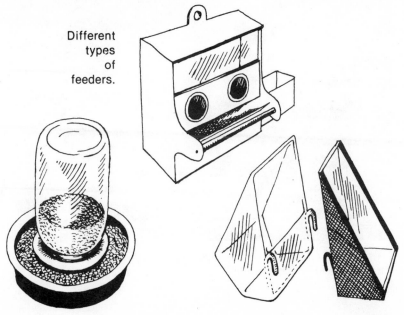

Different types of feeders.

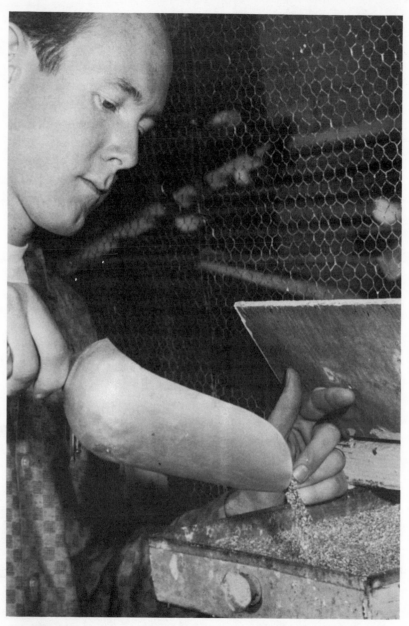

A practical aviary can be serviced from the outside. Here a pull-out tray for seeds is shown.

Chapter 13. Proper Management

The necessity of banding young zebra finches as well as other aviary birds was discussed in detail earlier, and something was said about the records that must be kept if one wishes to breed the birds in a responsible manner. In order to help you a bit with the management of your birds, here are several hints. Take a notebook and mark down everything that is, or seems to be, important. Each bird should have a section of its own in the notebook, because after some time has passed it is of inestimable value for the breeder to be able to refer to some item that will help him in his bird breeding. By systematically keeping up the records—and this is of the greatest importance—you can follow all the pairs to determine whether or not they were pure-bred, whether they were good or bad breeders, if they fed well, if they were argumentative and so forth. It is very possible that it will take several breeding seasons to build up a really comprehensive picture of all your birds.

The record can look something like the following. I have taken a page from one of my own zebra finch notebooks. You could improve, fill in or alter any part according to your own needs.

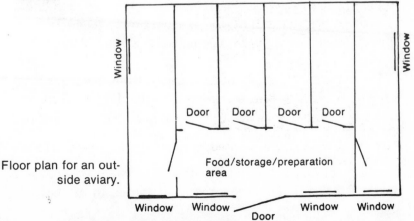

Floor plan for an out-
side aviary.

Housing:	Ring No. of male:	Ring No. of female:
Broodcage: 27	72-1977	38-1977

Outer coloring of male:
  Grey

Outer coloring of female:
  Grey

Ring color of male and female:
  Blue

Remarks:
To distinguish the parents from probable offspring, both of the adult zebra finches wear a color ring on the right foot.

Date of Hatching of Offspring:	*Ring No. of of Offspring:*	*Ring color:*
May 17, 1978	14-1978; 15-1978 17-1978; 18-1978 (No. 16-1978 died one week after leaving the nest)	Blue (left)

Color of Offspring:
14 grey (male)
15 grey (male)

16 grey (male) died
17 fawn-brown (female)
18 grey (male)

Special markings:
1. Outwardly normal grey zebra finch
2. Not homozygous according to appearance
3. Male parent carries fawn-brown line (no. 17 is fawn-brown female)
4. Female parent is a good breeding bird

You can draw a number of conclusions from the above information: fawn-brown is sex-linked; according to further breeding results the male is not pure grey but is of fawn-brown stock, which was already determined in the first brood: a fawn-brown female, No. 17. My second round of breeding showed in my records that there were two fawn-brown females. I then knew that if I wanted to get fawn-

122

brown males also, I would have to take the parent bird, for example, no. 72, and cross him with one of his daughters. Here, you see, we can consciously apply in-breeding. According to the laws of heredity which I will discuss in greater detail later, we should get fawn-brown males from this pairing, although they may not necessarily show up in the first round of breeding. This crossing will also produce fawn-brown females and normal grey males and females divided between fawn-brown and grey. But I am only concerned with the fawn-brown males, which will then be homozygous and from which I can breed a pure line. To understand how this works, read a little further in the book. I am fully aware that to many of you all of this still seems like just a lot of confusing talk, but it is only my intention here to show that it is of the utmost importance to keep complete and accurate records.

The use of filing cards is also good but requires a little more work. Each bird has its own card on which is listed all pertinent facts and occurrences. These cards can be stored in an index file or in boxes. You can buy the cards in any stationary store in a variety of colors and sizes or have cards cut to your own measurements.

These cards can also be placed in a notebook. On each card for each bird the following points can be listed:
Color; Date of Birth; Color of Mother; Ring No.; Color of Father; Ring No. of Mother; Ring color; Ring No. of Father; Date of Birth; Sex; Date of Birth; Ring color of Mother; Color of ring of Father; Heredity line; Special observations.

The more information recorded on the cards, the better you are able to determine the quality of the bird concerned. If you want to sell a particular bird about which everything is known, then the buyer only needs to check the card. He gets the card as a present and can continue to add notations as he continues with the breeding. Moreover, accurate card keeping can disclose a surprising picture of a bird, not only

Bengalese finches. In cases where the sexes are similar in color and/or size, such as in Bengalese, it is a difficult task to get a true pair. Experienced dealers and breeders get to know the cocks from the hens without really knowing any particular points of difference. Often a good dealer can pick out a pair for you.

The most abundant of all domesticated finches is the pretty and easily reared zebra finch, the 'leading character' of this book.

The long-tailed grass-finch is a beautiful little bird, though its hues are not brilliant, and it is seen to the best advantage in the aviary, where it is active and interesting.

concerning its genetic properties but also its relationship with birds of its own kind and with others, breeding performance, etc. At the same time you can distinguish the good from the less good. The *good* birds should never be sold arbitrarily, but only to devoted, enthusiastic breeders. People who take their zebra finch breeding seriously can efficiently carry on the good work and keep the birds and the breed from deteriorating.

African silverbill. This bird is very easy to breed in an aviary or large cage using the usual finch type nest box, with the entrance at one side. The domed nest is made of grass and feathers, etc.

Chapter 14. Sickness and Accidents

Birds are not easy creatures to cure when they fall sick, and some precautions are necessary if their well-being is to be maintained (consult *Bird Diseases* by L. Arnall and I.F. Keymer, a publication of TFH, Publ. Inc., Neptune, N.J.). One of the chief causes of ailments among foreign finches, including zebra finches, is fluctuating temperatures. Many birds from warm climates can withstand cold remarkably well, but a sudden drop in temperature, even in the height of summer, can start troublesome chills. Both in the bird-room and in the outdoor aviary, every precaution against drafts, damp and excessive heat or cold should be taken.

Cleanliness is also very important. Disease can be spread rapidly through drinking water allowed to remain contaminated with bird droppings. Fresh water daily should be the rule in the aviary, and it may be necessary to renew the water more frequently in the case of birds in cages and indoor aviaries.

Flying exercise, especially during the winter months, is essential to the health of birds, particularly those kept caged indoors. See that your cages have a good length, as this is more important than depth or height.

Always keep the floor of the cages clean and covered with sand on which cage bird grit is sprinkled. Remove all the stale green food or soft food at the end of the day. Do not give birds wet or partially frozen green food.

In spite of all precautions, birds will sometimes fall ill. The usual symptom is fluffed-out plumage, though this may be merely because the bird is feeling cold. The fancier soon learns to detect signs of trouble among his birds, and the important thing is to act at once. It is no use leaving a bird which seems to feel poorly among its companions. Neither will a sick bird which has eggs or young be any help to its

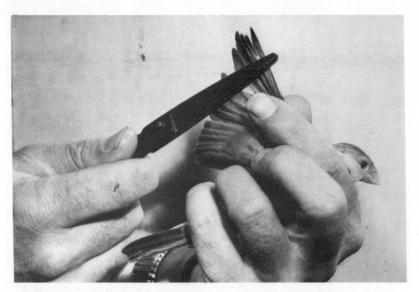

Clipping wings in an immature Java Rice Bird. For training, clip one wing. For reducing aggressiveness, clip both wings to provide a slowdown.

Strawberry finches, zebra finches and all species of nun finches customarily grow long toenails in aviaries with perches of too great a diameter. Clipping toenails is a simple task which gives the birds far more comfort and avoids dangerous entanglements in wire.

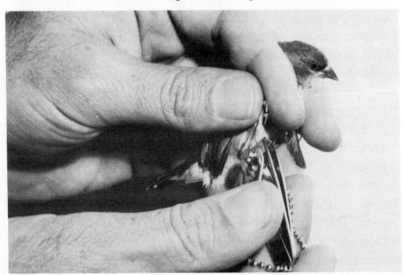

mate. There is only one rule with ailing birds— move them to a hospital cage.

Every fancier should have such a cage. Excellent types fitted with thermostatically controlled heaters are on the market, and you cannot do better than to buy one of these. A simple but quite useful hospital cage can be made from a wooden produce box. This should have a glass front, made to slip up and down, and a false metal floor. Under this is a heating element in the form of two or more forty-watt electric bulbs. It is best to have these arranged so that they can be switched on independently to control the amount of heat required. A cage should be fitted with a perch (not too high up) as well as with a small food and water container. It should also have a thermometer hung on the back wall where it can be easily read.

Heat is a prime necessity in curing sick birds. It is the only cure in most cases, and certainly one cannot do anything without it in the treatment of an egg-bound hen. Sometimes birds, especially young ones, which appear almost at the last gasp from exposure will revive if placed in the hospital cage at a temperature of around eighty degrees.

One last thought: all medicine should be given in water, in either glass or porcelain drinkers, never in metal.

Accidents

One of the most common accidents among birds is their habit of flying against glass window panes. This is especially the case with pet birds allowed to fly about the house. In the aviary and bird room all glass lights should be covered with half-inch wire netting. Birds will dash against glass substitutes when frightened, but we have personally not had any injured in this way, as the substitutes 'give' more easily and, of course, do not splinter if broken.

Broken legs sometimes occur from a bird having become caught by its claws in some portion of the wirework or fittings. If the break is at a joint little can be done and the leg

A large cage for one pair of zebra finches.

will always remain stiff. But, if broken at the shank bone, the injured limb may be set with the aid of splints. These should be cut from small strips of wood and made as light as possible. The splints should extend from the foot well up the thigh, but make sure that the upper ends are not long enough to injure the body of the bird during movement. Wrap the splints lightly in cotton and place them in position. Bind them firmly, but not too tightly, with a continuous wrapping of narrow, soft tape. Bird bones knit very quickly, and the best way to be sure it is time to remove the dressing is to watch the movements of the patient. When the bird appears to be perching well and gripping the support with the toes in a natural manner, the splints may be removed. Some stiffness of the limb remains for a while, but this will right itself eventually. A badly damaged broken leg in which the skin is torn and twisted should be amputated with a pair of sharp scissors. The stump soon heals.

Broken wings must be set in a natural position. Do not try to use splints. Instead, the two wings are bound to the body with a narrow tape dressing until the break has healed. This takes about ten days.

Apoplexy

This is often the cause of sudden death, and the bird may die too quickly for any form of treatment. Birds kept in cages that are too small, overfed and allowed insufficient exercise are most subject to this complaint. When an attack comes on, the victim becomes dizzy and falls to the ground with convulsed limbs. If you can get to the bird before it expires and plunge its head into a dish of water, it may recover. The patient should then be caged on its own and kept perfectly quiet for a few days.

Anemia

This sickness comes from poor housing and feeding. Insects can also be the cause of anemia. The color of the skin, bill and feet becomes lighter and the bird loses weight very quickly. The feeding and housing must be improved immediately. Jaundice (yellow-tinted skin color) often follows diarrhea and should be treated in the same way.

Even a breeding cage can be used as a hospital cage.

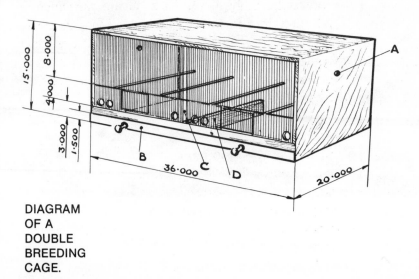

DIAGRAM
OF A
DOUBLE
BREEDING
CAGE.

131

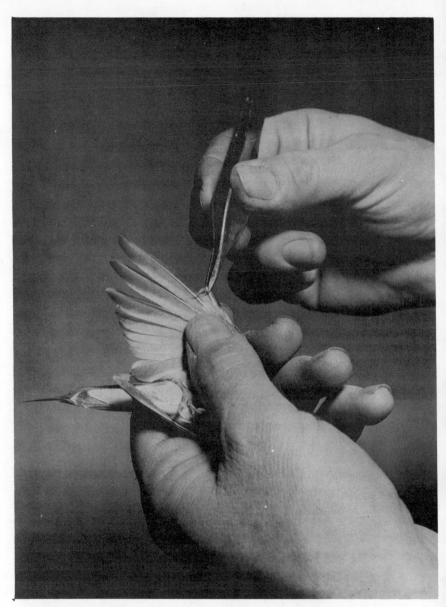

Removing broken stubs of wing feathers so new ones will grow quickly. Extracted feathers are replaced in six weeks, but natural regrowth through the molt may take six months.

Asthma

The symptoms of this are coughing, tightness of breath and weakness. Small doses of potassium bromide may be administered through the beak.

Bare of feathers

Some finches, particularly zebra finches and waxbill species, frequently lose their feathers, especially those of the head. This is common in newly-imported birds and can usually be cured by turning the birds into an outdoor aviary where they will receive direct sunlight. In winter this is not possible, but the addition to the drinking water of a little orange juice may effect a cure. The cause is generally too many rich, oily seeds which overload the system with food poisons, causing damage to the cell capillaries of the skin. Plenty of green food, especially dandelions and spinach, will put matters right.

Bare patches are also sometimes due to birds plucking each other. Some birds develop this vice when overcrowded, as when being imported, but give it up when turned into an aviary where they have other diversions. However, if the birds are kept in cages, offenders should be removed from other birds and caged by themselves.

Bronchitis

This is caused by inflammation of the bronchial tubes. The affected bird shows signs of weakness and labored breathing accompanied by a wheezing, rasping noise. Bad ventilation, exposure to damp and cold and sudden changes in temperature are all causes of this complaint. A generally effective mixture is glycerine, oxymel of squills and ipecac wine in equal quantities. Give half a teaspoon in drinking water.

Chalk legs or Scaly legs

Old birds are the worst sufferers from this. Smearing the legs with a mixture of vegetable oil and iodine generally takes care of the condition. A soda bath is good too. After treatment, spread petroleum jelly over the legs. Mites can also be the cause of the condition, in which case thoroughly disinfect the cage.

Chills

Birds get colds and chills in the same way as do humans—by drafts and sudden changes in temperature. They are more subject to the complaint if their resistance is in any way lowered. In winter, for instance, the long nights and short hours of daylight force many tropical species to take insufficient food. Artificial lighting in the aviary and bird-room will enable this trouble to be overcome. A bird suffering from a chill sits puffed up, often with shivering wings. There may be fluid running from the nostrils. Heat is the main remedy; the bird should be placed in the hospital cage at a temperature of not less than eighty degrees Fahrenheit for a few hours. If the bird seems to be less distressed, the temperature may be gradually lowered. Birds brought inside from outdoor quarters in winter and suffering from chills should not be put outside again until spring.

Coccidiosis

This disease is caused by parasites in the intestine which set up inflammation or enteritis. It runs a rapid course, killing in two or three days. The symptoms are fluffed-out plumage, restlessness and sometimes diarrhea. Death generally takes place during an attack of convulsions. The corpse is usually emaciated. The disease is most prevalent in early summer and is contagious. Cages in which the birds known to be suffering from coccidiosis have been kept should be thoroughly cleaned with boiling water containing caustic soda, and it might be a good idea to go over the metal cages with a blowtorch. Tincture of catechu should be given in the drinking water, about five drops to every teaspoon of water; this should be continued for several days.

Constipation

This is not an uncommon trouble among birds. The chief symptom is a frequent attempt to evacuate without results. A good old remedy is to add ten drops of syrup of buckthorn to a drinker of water. A very small pinch of Glauber's salt in the drinking water is also recommended. Birds suffering from constipation should be encouraged to eat green food, seeding grasses and millet seed soaked until it begins to sprout.

Diarrhea

There are very many possible causes of diarrhea or enteritis, and it can be mild or serious to a fatal degree. Diarrhea may be caused or abetted by viruses, decomposed foods, poisonous plants, bacteria, protozoa, etc. Chills may predispose birds to develop the complaint. It can also be readily brought on in birds from fright in catching them or by sudden changes in food. Young, immature and freshly acquired birds are more liable to it. Stale egg-food is a sure and deadly cause of enteritis. Dirty or infected cages, dirty food and water vessels and moldly or dusty seeds are all possible causes of the trouble. Sudden climatic change will often bring on an attack of diarrhea in tropical finches, as it lowers the resistance of the birds. Lack of suitable grit is a common cause of diarrhea from digestive troubles.

Birds suffering from the trouble have the undertail feathers soiled, and their droppings may be watery. Sufferers should be kept warm, as warmth alone often cures a bird. A few drops of chlorodyne in the drinking water is the safest medicine to give.

Egg-binding

This is easily the most troublesome ailment of the breeding aviary, and probably more hen birds are lost through it than any other cause. Egg-binding is really a cramp of the oviduct and occurs most frequently during wet and chilly weather. The bird invariably leaves her nest and sits on the floor fluffed-up and in pain. She can seldom fly more than a few feet and may crouch in a corner. Heat is the only cure. If the bird is gently caught and placed in a box before a fire, or better still in a hospital cage heated to about eighty-five or ninety degrees Fahrenheit, the chances are she will quickly recover. The egg should be laid within a few hours, and the bird must not be returned to her cage or aviary until this has taken place. She will rarely take any further interest in sitting for some weeks. Some fanciers make a practice of anointing the vent with olive oil, using a camel's hair brush for the purpose, while others believe in holding the bird over a jug of boiling water. But the writer has had very satisfactory results simply by putting the birds in a cage and maintaining a steady heat. Give seeds and water, as the bird will take this as soon as the pain from the cramp is relieved by the warmth.

Sometimes a hen is egg-bound with the first egg of her second clutch, though it is generally the first egg of the season which causes the trouble. Some hens are more prone to the trouble than others. One cause of egg-binding is the lack of a shell on the egg, in which case the muscles cannot properly expel it. See that your birds have a plentiful supply of suitable shell grit and cuttlebone. Slaked garden lime may be put in their bath and drinking water, especially if your water supply is of the 'soft' type.

Inflamed eyes

This affliction occurs mostly in the winter months and is due to a vitamin deficiency. Give lettuce and oil-bearing

136

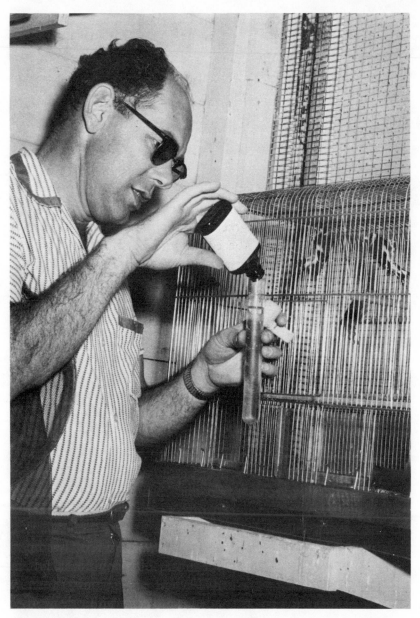

Adding vitamins to the drinking water stimulates the appetite of our birds.

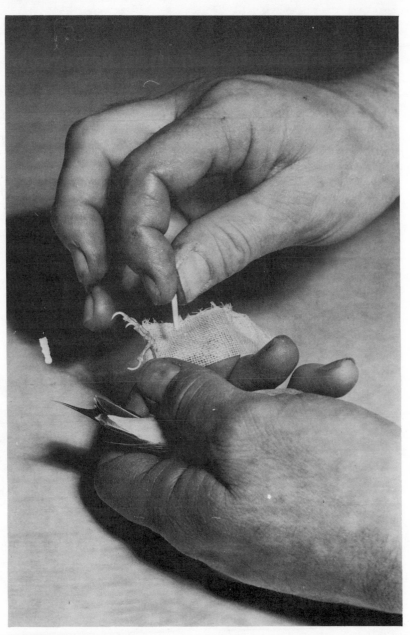

Broken bones knit rapidly in birds, and usually a week's recuperation will clear up all debility from a broken leg.

seeds and mix some cod-liver oil in with the seeds.

Inflamed oil-gland

The oil-gland, located at the base of the tail, can become inflamed when the bird does not have enough room to fly about or cannot wash itself vigorously. A little vegetable oil placed under the tail can help considerably.

Parasites

Birds are unfortunately subject to many parasites. As far as cage and aviary specimens are concerned, only mites are likely to be a source of trouble. Of these, red mites are the most troublesome pest. These mites suck the blood of the birds at night, leaving the victims in the daytime and hiding in cracks in the woodwork, in the slits at the ends of the perches, or, in ornamental metal cages, in the metal dome at the top of the cage. A metal cage can be rid of these mites with the aid of boiling water. Wooden cages and nest boxes should be treated with liquid household disinfectant. If a dark color is not objected to, there is nothing better than creosote for keeping red mites in check.

Feather mites live on the birds and do not leave their hosts regularly as do red mites. They are tiny greyish creatures which irritate the birds and in bad cases cause ragged plumage. Treatment consists of dusting the plumage of affected birds with insect powder, a safe kind being derris dust as used by gardeners; or you can use flowers of sulphur.

Two young zebra finches with their proud father!

II. HEREDITY AND CROSSING

Chapter 1. How Did The Breeding Of Zebra Finches Develop?

It is, of course, not news to the bird breeder that by the systematic breeding of particular birds, variations are obtained, some of which are so radical that it would be justified to speak of a new strain. You need only to go to a poultry show to see this with your own eyes. Therefore, it is not surprising that zebra finches also show many differences. There are any number of color strains to be seen in the bird shops and at various breeders.

We will discuss color-breeding variations in some detail since the interest in zebra finches has increased greatly since the Second World War. There are now a number of national and international zebra finch clubs. The forming of bird clubs with the object of breeding and caring for a particular variety of bird is not a fad among a few bird keepers; it is a real necessity if you wish to attain any reasonable degree of specialization. A breeder working alone cannot undertake a breeding program large enough to exert an influence upon the further breeding of a particular variety, but by working collectively, breeders can anticipate the appearance of certain deviations and exert some control over them.
some control over them.

As an example of the results achieved in conjunction with a club, we can compare the canary and budgerigar clubs. The budgerigar or parrakeet was one of the first birds for which a club was established. Around 1920 there were only two, or at most three, mutations. In England, the land of parrakeet breeders, a club decided to specialize and achieved amazing results. The breeding of parrakeets in England is

In this cage the birds are exposed on all sides and there is really no place in which they can find seclusion. A zebra finch, when approached, will most likely panic. To avoid this, place an open cage close to a wall to provide it with a solid back, although you will lose much of the apparent virtue of an all-wire cage.

now a well-established branch of the hobby of bird raising, with meticulously defined standard types and a wealth of knowledge about the bird.

Whenever I attempt to compare the standards demanded in the U.S.A. with those that the English make for their regional and national shows, I feel ashamed. During one of my visits to the annual parrakeet exhibition in Bradfort, England, held by the Bradfort Budgerigar Society, I came to the disquieting conclusion that the worst entries there would easily win a first prize in our country or perhaps even capture an honor or champion title. Fortunately the level of breeding in our country is rising, although many breeders still lack sufficient knowledge about heredity and cross-breeding as well as the care and housing of the birds. If we want to reach the level of the British, we must work more intensively and with greater dedication.

The breeding of zebra finches is still at its early stages. In England, the breeders are a bit ahead of us here in the States, but this is not terribly important. As far as I could determine, our English counterparts are also in the early stages of development. This could hardly be otherwise in view of the fact that the zebra finch is now being systematically bred for the first time, while the parrakeet had already been bred to an overwhelming wealth of colors and markings as early as the 1920's. Before the Second World War, the average breeder of zebra finches bred this bird just as he did any other tropical bird and was not aware of the many possibilities it offered. But once the development of the zebra finch started, the connoisseurs and judges were confronted with the same experiences that must have faced the parrakeet judges. At exhibitions zebra finches of the normal grey wild color were shown, but those that deviated in color and form

An all-wire cage affords little protection to the birds from drafts which can be, and often are, fatal.

143

Several of the lovliest and most ideal of all finches in aviculture come from Australia. Unfortunately all except zebra finches are becoming increasingly scarce.

were startling to the eye. There were birds with completely black breasts, as well as some with scant markings; some had stripes along the base of the bill and cheek patch that formed a black triangle; and others had black breast markings. In short, they presented a staggering amount of "new" material. The new variations aroused an enormous amount of interest, but knowledge concerning breeding methods and how to expect particular kinds of offspring was slow in developing.

The American zebra finch expert, Mathew Bender, had during this time envisioned the danger of a too general, chaotic breeding for color, and he warned against it. He wrote out a large questionnaire for breeders breeding their birds in the usual way and, from the accumulated breeding results, put together a correct table of hereditary factors. After finishing this long and meritorious task (the table lists about 500 pairing combinations), he had to come to the conclusion that the table was far from complete. Indeed, the difficult new mutations such as penguins, white-heads and multicolor are missing.

Meanwhile, we are now a few years further on and can confidently say that the zebra finch can look forward to a bright future. We have had at our disposal for some years now birds that have been bred in our own land. Although the value of bringing in birds from Australia as "fresh blood" cannot be discounted, we can certainly help any interested breeder with our home-bred material.

The normal grey zebra finch—the wild color—should be identical with the original Australian form or approach it as closely as possible; degeneration quickly leads to disaster. Therefore, it is probably worthwhile to give a detailed description of the real wild bird in nature. First of all, it must have a good strong body build. There are ornithologists who believe that there are substantial differences among zebra finches in the wild, not only in size but also in

Zebra finches are very prolific and so are very plentiful and inexpensive, unlike many other Australian finch species.

An indoor aviary with a variety of tropical birds, among them zebra finches and Java rice birds.

A trio of golden-breasted waxbills. These tiny birds make a colorful addition to any collection. They are quite harmless and fairly good breeders, but it is not always easy to rear the young birds to adulthood. The birds will line the nestbox with feathers, which should be scattered about the aviary floor for this purpose.

color and markings. I have noted that the zebra finches from northwestern Australia have a somewhat different form than those from the southern areas, but there is certainly not sufficient difference to speak of a different subspecies. There is also some difference in coloration; those from the northwest are of a lighter shade than birds from the south, but here, too, the difference is negligible.

Bird experts, and in particular G.M. Mathews, at one time divided zebra finches into no fewer than seven subspecies. He began with several features he considered worthy of note, such as the color of the bill, the size and color of the cheek or ear patch, the intensity of the black band on the breast of the male and strength of the grey color on the back. However, in the introduction we saw that Keast demonstrated the opposite, so at the moment we distinguish only one sort, not

taking into consideration the birds from Timor. The differences that Mathews and others pointed out lead back to certain details that are often ignored: climate, food and other environmental circumstances. These often cause zebra finches—and other kinds of birds—to "degenerate," but these circumstances certainly do not beget separate kinds!

In our "normal" bird, the feathers must close tightly and the bill and feet should be coral red. The somewhat egg-shaped ear patches must be chestnut brown, with the front side bordered by a vertical black stripe. The same kind of stripe should be found along the base of the beak. The ear patch and the bill stripe should run toward each other under the head. It is important that the breast markings—"zebra markings"—be even, and on the underside there should be a black band. A completely black chest is definitely not desirable. The part of the sides that is covered by the wings should be chestnut brown with evenly spaced white spots all of the same size and lying in a row. The markings of the upper side of the tail must be only black and white. Many birds have spotted markings on the head and rich black markings on the breast. This is not good and it would be advisable to stop using such birds for breeding.

The female has no side markings; the breast pattern and ear patch are also missing. The feet and bill are a good red but lighter than those of the male. This, however, is not always the case; the feet and bill of male and female white zebra finches are virtually indistinguishable. Grey females can have darker breast markings without those markings being considered objectionable.

Opposite: A large flight cage for finches. This cage is on rollers so that it can easily be moved.

Finches are usually small birds ranging from three to six inches in length. They are mainly dependent upon seeds as the major source of their foods and are therefore called hardbills as opposed to soft-bills, which live mainly upon soft fruits and insects.

Chapter 2. Introduction to Heredity

Let us suppose that you are an advanced bird keeper, someone who knows what the birds require in the way of food and housing and knows how to care for them if they become sick. But now you are interested in the heredity and crossing factors of breeding. You had been convinced that if you paired a couple of white zebra finches you would produce white offspring, and that the same went for other color variations and mutations. You were brimming with enthusiasm about your experiments until you found, to your amazement, that you had bred a clutch of two grey and three white zebra finches. That struck you as most peculiar, because other breeders could tell you most accurately the kind of offspring they could expect from a particular couple. To clarify this a bit, let me explain to you some principles of genetics.

We all know that most living creatures originate from the joining of an egg cell from the mother and a sperm cell from the father. The cell that results from this fusion is called a zygote. This zygote goes through a developmental period until a new organism is formed. The higher forms of plant and animal life, including man (we will not concern ourselves with the one cell animals and plants), consist of millions of cells, all of which originated from a zygote. The enormous number of cells comes through cell division: the zygote divides into two and, when these two have matured, they each divide in two, and so it goes. The bird egg also develops from a cell and forms a protective layer of lime. The offspring emerges from the egg at hatching and continues to develop further as its cells continue to divide again.

But let us turn back to the first cells gotten from the mother and father, the egg and sperm cells. These are reproductive cells called gametes. These gametes possess the

The cut-throat or ribbon finch gets its name from the red bar found across the throat.

heredity factors that are present in the male and female. In the nucleus of the cell are small bodies known as *chromosomes* that carry chemical units called the *genes* whose function is specifically concerned with the passing on of heredity factors. The chromosomes, which are themselves divided into pairs, determine what manifestations will come forth in the new organism. When a cell gets ready to divide, the chromosomes also divide so that each cell always gets an equal number of chromosomes. The gametes each have only *one half* the number of chromosomes of body cells. If this were not so, the fusion of the egg cell and the sperm cell would produce double the number of chromosomes.

I will give an example to make this clear: if the body cells have 18 chromosomes, then the egg cell from the female has nine and the sperm cell from the male has nine. The joining of these two cells produces a zygote that obviously has eighteen chromosomes. The zygote then, after a period of time, divides normally, as we described before. In other words: we get one division after another of 2, 4, 8, 16, 32, 64, 128, 256, 512, 1024, 2048, 4096 cells, etc., each of which has 18 chromosomes.

The young zebra finch gets hereditary qualities from the female as well as the male, half from the father bird and half from the mother bird. This does not mean that the crossing of two colors will provide a combination of those two colors. We must deal with the invisible and visible factors which are known as the *recessive* (or subordinate) and *dominant* factors respectively. Both factors are of the greatest importance in dealing with the heredity of zebra finches; a particular color can completely overpower another color.

Indian spice or nutmeg finch. This is one of the best-known species of all finches and is always available, although it is difficult to obtain a true pair. Should a pair begin to nest, they must be given absolute quiet. Any slight disturbance could seriously hamper breeding attempts, and success would be doubtful.

153

As an example, let us take a white bird and a grey bird, both of which are pure bred (homozygous). When we cross these birds we will get visually grey offspring carrying the recessive white factor, which is invisible. We do not get grey offspring flecked with white or various combinations of white and grey. The grey factor is dominant, producing grey birds, while the white remains recessive. The grey offspring are registered by the breeders as normal/white zebra finches, the diagonal line (/) indicating that these birds are not pure-bred but are "split" (or carrying) for the white gene. If we cross one of these offspring with another bird carrying the white recessive gene, we have a 25% chance of getting pure-bred white birds because the white recessive gene is in both parents and consequently the grey factor is to a degree pushed aside or superseded.

Melba finch. Only experienced fanciers should attempt to keep these delicate South African birds, as their acclimation is difficult and requires much attention.

Homozygous and Heterozygous

Now that we know a bit more about zygotes, genes and chromosomes, we can broaden our knowledge a little more. We already know that when we breed birds of particular colors we do not necessarily get offspring of the same colors. We saw that the crossing of white and grey did not produce grey-whites or white-greys. This was due to the fact that certain factors (white for example) were recessive and only the dominant factor (grey) was visible.

There are untold numbers of birds possessing hidden color possibilities beneath their external colors. Such birds originate when we cross two birds of different colors, thus endowing the offspring with a variety of colors, both visible and invisible, from their parents. Such a non-pure-bred bird is said to be *heterozygous*.

To illustrate the above, here is an example. We saw that the crossing of white x grey produced completely grey young with a latent white gene, that is, split for white. Now, if we cross white x grey/white, we get 50% homozygous or pure-bred white birds because the white factor is very strongly present; the father is pure white and the mother is split. This crossing will also produce 50% grey birds which are split for white. If we pair greys that are split for white, the grey will be dominant again over the white, which gave us the result we saw; at least 50% of the birds are grey split for white (heterozygous); 25% are pure-bred grey (homozygous) and 25% are pure-bred white (homozygous). Perhaps this result seems strange to you, but I use this example only to show you how strongly a particular color can dominate and that what may appear to the eye to be pure-bred birds could turn out on breeding to be heterozygous birds.

The opposite of heterozygous is *homozygous*, a term we do not have to clarify further since it was illustrated in the example. For the sake of further clarity, the following should be noted: homozygous animals are pure-bred for a particular character. If we have a homozygous zebra finch, then this

1. Black-headed and white-headed mannikins, small finches with large beaks and coarse feet, but close and sleek plumage of plain but pleasing colors. 2. The Bengalese finch was originally produced many centuries ago by the Chinese and is believed to have resulted from a cross between the striated finch and the sharp-tailed finch.

Bengalese finches are difficult to sex by observation. In most mannikins the males have larger beaks than do the females.

bird will possess no other qualities or characters than those we observe from its outward appearance. It is completely understandable that non-pure birds and pure-bred birds may sometimes be outwardly indistinguishable from one another. From the crossing of white x grey/white for example, we saw 50% grey/white offspring which looked exactly like homozygous grey zebra finches, but when we cross these birds possessing latent or recessive white, a certain percentage of their offspring will show the white.

Societies nest as well in cages as they do in aviaries. They are ideal foster parents for many of the rarer finches which are more difficult to breed.

When we cross two homozygous birds of the same color, we can expect pure color offspring. A crossing of homozygous silverwings (male and female) will produce silverwinged homozygous young. This cannot miss, for the parents cannot pass on any color they do not possess (grey, white or cream, for example). The parents are pure-bred, and we can in turn expect 100% pure-bred offspring.

Actually it is not too easy to come by a homozygous pair. Most breeders are not that careful about keeping differently colored birds from breeding with each other. For the most part, it is practically impossible to trace the hereditary line of the different offspring to determine whether or not all the crossings have indeed been with pure-bred birds. We can only be certain by personally keeping close control of the couple and their offspring. This is almost impossible in a colony breeding cage or an aviary unless we populate it only with homozygous pairs of one color. However, it can be done more easily in one brooding cage.

Mendel's Theory

Whenever we speak of heredity and crossing, we frequently use the word "Mendelian." Any knowledgeable bird breeder can tell you that this word comes from Gregor Mendel, the name of the priest-biologist who experimented primarily with garden crops. But who was he actually?

Gregor Johann Mendel was born in Heinzendorf, Austria in 1822. When he was twenty-one he entered the Augustinian Monastery at Brünn (Brno, Czechoslovakia), where he was made a priest in 1847. From 1851 to 1853 he studied natural science in Vienna and then returned to the monastery. In 1868 he was made abbot of the monastery, where he continued his experiments for many years. When he died in 1884 he was honored as a fine abbot of the monastery, but he was completely unknown as a scientist who laid the foundation for the whole theory of heredity. Only years later was the intrinsic value of his work appreciated and recognized.

Mendel started his experiments in 1865 with the common garden pea. He chose this legume because it had the advantage of providing a great number of seedlings in each generation and he could accurately observe the relationships between the various types and their hereditary factors. By pollenating two like plants himself, he could tell whether the new plant that appeared was pure-bred or not.

Mendel published his research and discoveries in publications of the Brünn Society for the Study of Natural Science in 1865, but it was not until 1900 that De Vries of the Netherlands, Tschermak of Austria and Correns of Germany discovered Mendel's work and gave it the prominence and appreciation it deserved.

Briefly stated, here are the laws of Mendel:

1. In principle the male and female sex cells are especially equipped to pass on hereditary characters, which means that it makes no difference if a particular character comes from the mother or the father.

2. The sex cells are pure-bred and therefore cannot possess a deviating character. In other words, when the sex cells divide they do not contain pairs of chromosomes. They have only one chromosome from each pair. One sperm cell or one egg cell can pass on only one character from each pair of chromosomes.

3. Heredity embraces a number of tendencies (the Danish plant expert Johannsen, 1857-1927, spoke of "genes" in connection with this) that work independently of one another.

Meanwhile it has become clear that from the point of view of genetics, when we say white, fawn-brown, etc. the color actually is *pure* white, *pure* fawn-brown etc. In other words, we are speaking of colored birds that we know to be homozygous, pure-bred for a particular character. On the other hand, if a heterozygous (not pure-bred) bird is bred for a particular quality, then for the sake of convenience it is listed by the visible color as well as its recessive or invisible color. A heterozygous bird that is outwardly white but car-

Clockwise: two crested gray males and one (young) crested gray female.

ries grey would be classified as a white/grey bird or a "white-blooded" zebra finch, which means "white out of grey." No matter what we call it, the meaning is now clear. The different names can well lead to confusion, so I will stick to the terminology generally used in bird breeding literature—the English term *split*. In our example then, we have white split grey (white/grey).

Is In-breeding Useful or Dangerous?

I believe that the word *in-breeding* arouses negative feelings in a great many bird breeders. In-breeding is often wrong and can be very seriously wrong because, as is claimed, it can result in sick, weak and defective birds.

Indeed, we often see defects in birds that have been in-bred, but we must carefully sort out and identify the causes. You have read that older birds pass on a particular character (shape, color, song) to the offspring. A completely new bird of different blood could transmit a particular character, good or bad. If we now cross an old bird having a bad character (or hidden tendency for the bad character) with another bird having the same bad character or tendency to it, then the chance of passing it on is sharply increased. If these birds are closely related it will almost certainly show up in the close confines of the family. The offspring will have the bad quality not because of the in-breeding as such, but because both the mother and father transmitted the bad trait. We do not speak of in-breeding within the extended family; only the offspring of father-daughter, mother-son, brother-sister and niece-nephew are considered in-bred. Many breeders do not include niece-nephew.

Suppose that we breed with *good* birds, well raised, well selected, without defects, well built and of the desired color; moreover, we are fully aware of the recessive or hidden characters (split). If this is the case, there is no need to fear in-breeding, and it can even be very useful and necessary. It

Silver zebra finches are marked like gray zebras, but they have a pale silver-gray replacing the darker areas of the gray zebra. Usually the price is low on this color variety.

is certainly useful in helping us reach our goal more surely and more quickly (for example, a particular color variation), and it can be necessary if we want to hold on to a particular mutation. For example: we would like to breed a pair of white zebra finches. This is a simple situation. We pair a male white zebra finch, known to us to be pure-bred, with a grey female. The offspring are grey birds split for white (grey/white). Then comes the in-breeding. We take the white male, *the father*, and pair him with a grey/white female, *a daughter*. This produces 50% pure white birds and 50% greys split for white. You obtained a white couple after only two crossings, only requiring a homozygous male. This male when paired with a white female (a daughter) produces 100% white offspring. It should be understood, however, that the young from this white x white crossing will not con-

Above: two penguin crested females (back and side) *Below:* two dominant blackbreast gray males (back and front).

Above: two brown males (front and back); inset: brown male with a yellow bill. Below: two young variegated males (back and front).

tinue to be good breeding birds because there will have been more than enough in-breeding. It makes sense to set up two parallel breeding lines. Then it will not be necessary to make extensive use of in-breeding, since couples can be chosen from the white males and white females coming from two separate families.

A few words about mutation: when there suddenly appears a complete change in color or shape in a plant or animal that cannot be accounted for by the laws of heredity, we speak of a *mutation*. Through a change in the hereditary composition

In mixed aviaries Bengalese and zebra finches are overly helpful in community nesting operations. They frequently move in with any bird who happens to be nesting!

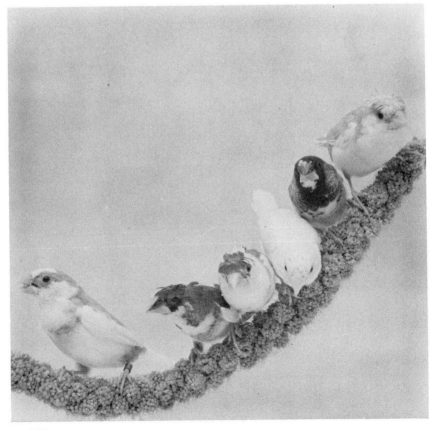

of the chromosomes, the causes of which are for the most part unknown, there can suddenly appear a color and/or shape deviation. This can be done intentionally in some cases but it usually occurs spontaneously. Mutation should not be confused with *modifications*. There are certain foods that can be fed to birds to alter their color, such as that used by canary breeders to make their red birds a deeper shade of red. Then too, the lack of certain substances such as vitamins can cause a change in the bird, but these changes disappear when the correct diet is restored or, as in the case of the "color food," taken away. Mutations are inheritable while modifications are not. For example, if our canary breeders stop feeding their red birds the particular food that intensifies their color, the birds become paler. If two birds which have been fed the color-inducing food are paired, they most decidedly will not produce deep red offspring!

Here is an example of how a mutation can be perpetuated by in-breeding. After a breeding, a mutation is discovered—perhaps a fawn-brown with a red tail. The pair is homozygous, which tells us it is not split for any other color. The mutant is a female. Now let us suppose that the mutation came from the male. We would then pair the same male with the mutant and produce some offspring with the mutation; fawn-brown with red tail has a 50% chance of appearing. If it turns out that the original father was not the source of the mutation, we must continue a bit longer with one more breeding. With the first pairing of father and daughter there existed, along with the 50% fawn-brown offspring, also 50% of the offspring that are split for the mutation (mutation-carrying). If a male offspring from this pair is now coupled with the original mother, the source of the mutation, then we will again get birds showing the mutation. I hope that through these examples you can overcome your aversion to the word "in-breeding" and come to realize that, in pursuit of our interest in bird breeding, it often plays a useful as well as necessary role.

All different varieties of Bengalese finches, all with a double crest. *Upper photos:* light brown (back and front). *Lower photos:* cinnamon (back and front).

Above: dark brown crested (back and front). *Below:* white variegated crested (back and front).

The bronze-winged mannikin is a rather small bird and is a suitable companion for Java sparrows and weavers; it has bred in an aviary. It is hardy but has the reputation of being a bully, which is an overstatement.

Sex and Sex-linked Inheritance

Before we look further into known mutations and color varieties I would like to call your attention to a very important aspect of breeding for color, namely sex-linked heredity.

From what has been said already, you understand that the sex of the bird is determined by the *genes* (the carriers of the hereditary factors in the chromosomes). The female zebra finch has two sex-determining chromosomes, namely one X-chromosome, or male chromosome, and one Y-chromosome, or female chromosome. The male zebra finch also has two sex chromosomes, one X-chromosome, or male chromosome, and another X, or male chromosome. The sex difference between the female and the male lies solely in the fact that the female carries both a male and a female chromosome while the male carries only male chromosomes. In the joining of a male chromosome from the female with a male chromosome from the male (he can give no other), we get a male offspring. Schematically we can show this very simply: Male X-chromosome + female X-chromosome = 2 X-chromosomes = male. Another possibility is a Y-chromosome from the female with the X-chromosome from the male, resulting in a female offspring. Schematically it looks like this: Male X-chromosome + Female Y-chromosome = X + Y chromosomes = female. Thus we can see that the female and not the male determines the sex of the offspring.

However, our explanation of sex-related heredity does not end with the discussion of sex determination. Another factor that is sex-related is that of color. When you are sure a definite relationship between the color factor and sex chromosomes exists, then you must think of sex-linked heredity. Here the sex is in direct relationship to definite observable qualities of the zebra finch. The sex is bound in with the specific marking or markings you wish to obtain from the bird you are going to cross. You must understand that not every bird passes on sex-related heredity factors; in the case of zebra finches, for instance, black mask, black back, fawn-brown and cream are sex-bound. In the female the factors for black mask, black back, fawn-brown and cream are missing, therefore females cannot inherit black mask, black back, fawn-brown or cream as a split factor. Only males are *split* for these colors.

Equipment for aviaries consists, for example, of perches, waterers, baths, feeders, nest-boxes, etc. There is much choice and variation. Ask your pet shop for professional advice.

An all-bamboo ornamental cage. This type is very popular with those fanciers who keep just one or two birds as livingroom pets, but they are unpopular with serious birdlovers.

The relatively inexpensive gray zebra finch is the original (wild) variety.

Chapter 3. Crossings

Grey, the normal or wild colored zebra finch

The normal grey color is dominant over all factors with the exception of the silver factor; grey is recessive to dominant silver. We know, of course, of grey zebra finches that are normal but are split for one or more factors even though they appear outwardly to be normal grey birds. In captivity as well as in the wild, we find various tints of grey. The light grey is of interest to us because it indicates the presence of silver or white. This factor is naturally split. If we want to breed a light grey zebra finch, we proceed in the following manner. By crossing a grey x white, we get a grey bird with white as a split factor. The second generation—called F_2—we cross a grey/white x pure white (homozygous) and produce 50% white and 50% grey split white offspring. For the rest, it is understandable that these last birds, the split white zebra finches, should be crossed with white rather than the young from the grey x white crossing of the first generation. From this point on, do not breed these two crossings any further! Breed the same birds only to two generations; if you continue to breed them further you will see offspring with color deviations and perhaps even defective shapes.

The normal grey can also be split fawn-brown as well as split white. In this case the sex relationship becomes apparent. The fawn-brown factor is sex-linked, so the females cannot be split for another color and only the males can be split for the fawn-brown factor. There can only be grey/fawn-brown and grey/white males (the sign / stands for split, as you know). With the information we have now, we can make an outline:

Grey males can be: a) grey; b) grey split for white; c) grey split for fawn-brown and d) grey split for fawn-brown and white. These four colors are all grey and cannot be (or can

The author's aviaries for all kinds of finches, offering all the comforts known to these birds in their natural habitat. Notice the attractive as well as sturdy construction of these aviaries. A common fault with beginners is that of overcrowding their aviaries. Where breeding results are especially desired the number of pairs must be strictly limited . . . according to color!

A male zebra finch belonging to what ornithologists call "grass-finches." This term embraces the graceful, colorful Australian finches, which together with the parrot finches form a most important group of aviary birds.

only barely be) distinguished from one another. For the sake of completeness, I will give the possibilities of a grey female. These are quite scant, as we know: grey females can be: a) normal grey and b) grey/white. Therefore, next to the normal wild color the only possibility is grey/white.

It is important to know that *white is recessive to grey and fawn-brown.* In crossing white (male) x grey (female), the offspring are grey but split for white. Grey x fawn-brown results in grey males split for fawn-brown and grey females.

When we pair the young from the white x grey crossing, we get a combination of grey/white x grey/white. The result gives us a certain percentage of grey females and males (16.67 per 100 birds); further, we get 16.67% white females and white males split for grey *with black eyes* and finally, 16.67% grey/white females and males.

If we cross a grey male split for white with a normal grey female in which there is no white factor (homozygous) the result will be totally grey offspring, both males and females, at least outwardly. 50% of these birds are split for white. Now we can breed white birds with black eyes and, similarly, with red eyes (albinos; birds having a brown factor about which we will speak later). The zebra finches that are white with red eyes are not totally albino because they have retained their original red bills and red feet. Birds are albinos when their bills and feet are colorless; albinos lack all pigment. The name *albino finch* is actually wrong, and in its place I will use the name *pseudo-albino finch*.

Zebra finches in their many color varieties are more eagerly sought after by aviculturists than any other group of finches!

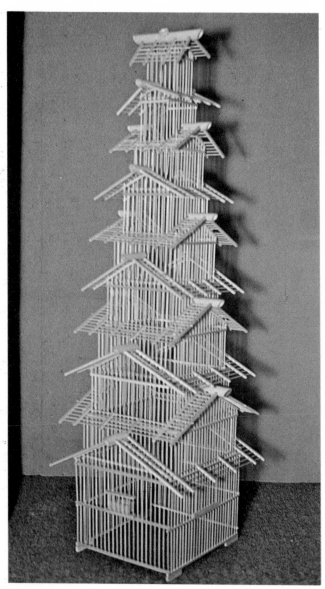

Oriental cage for a few pairs of zebra finches; although
very attractive in appearance, such cages are regarded
by most fanciers as inadequate.

The zebra finch is the best-known of all Australian finches and is a perky, hardy, pompous little bird with a ridiculous song sounding like the piping of a toy whistle. Several pairs (but never two!) will live amicably together and breed in an aviary, but in this case there should be nesting boxes to spare, otherwise pairs may select the same box and waste most of the breeding season bickering over its possession.

181

Do not put zebra finches in an outside aviary until late spring, when the cold weather is well past.

In addition to the black and red eyes, we meet another color deviation, the *black-brown*, which lies between black and red (or brown if you prefer to call it that). White animals with deep black eyes carry the black factor, and those with red eyes carry the brown factor. Intermediate birds carry both black and brown factors. These last-mentioned birds are extremely interesting because both factors become completely apparent when the birds are crossed with zebra finches which are any color but white. If, for example, a fawn-brown female is crossed with a white zebra finch male having black eyes, we get grey males and grey females. The males, as you now know, are split for white and split for

Aviary bred and acclimated zebras are fairly hardy, but in England and similar climates they are best brought indoors from about the end of October until spring.

fawn-brown; the females are split for white (fawn-brown, you remember, is sex-related).

Perhaps it will be useful to see several tables showing the different relationships between grey, fawn-brown and white. The percentages only make good sense if you figure on a large scale of 100 birds. It is quite common that in a nest of four grey birds only one seems to fit the rules.

1. Normal grey x normal grey gives:
100%—normal grey males and females

2. Normal grey x grey/white gives:
25%—grey males
25%—grey females
25%—grey/white males
25%—grey/white females

A male white zebra finch. White zebras were first bred by Mr. A.J. Woods, of Sydney, Australia, who reared three young ones in an aviary containing a mixed collection in 1921. They were later established by another Sydney fancier, Mr. H. Lyons, who obtained his initial stock from Mr. Woods.

A female brown wing. Color variations of zebras have turned up before the white mutations, and even Dr. Russ, the German aviculturist of the nineteenth century, mentions some colors, like white and brown. Russ, however, attached no importance to these sports and did not attempt to retain them by line breeding. The brown wings appeared in the '60's.

A so-called 'dual-sexed' bird. Color and markings on the right side are different from those on the left. Shown is the "male" side.

3. Normal grey x fawn-brown gives:
50%—grey/fawn-brown males
50%—grey females

4. Normal grey x fawn-brown/white gives:
25%—grey/fawn-brown males
25%—grey females
25%—grey/fawn-brown/white males
25%—grey/white females

5. Grey/fawn-brown x normal grey gives:
25%—grey males
25%—grey females
25%—grey/fawn-brown males
25%—fawn-brown females

6. Grey/fawn-brown x grey/white gives:

12½%—grey males
12½%—grey females
12½%—grey/fawn-brown males
12½%—grey/white females
12½%—grey/white males
12½%—fawn-brown females
12½%—grey/fawn-brown/white males
12½%—fawn-brown/white females

7. Grey/fawn-brown x fawn-brown gives:

25%—grey/fawn-brown males
25%—fawn-brown males
50%—fawn-brown females

The other side of the 'dual-sexed', a rare mutation. This is the "female" side.

A silver male zebra finch. It is not unusual when a race of birds starts
to mutate that a dilution character occurs, and this is so with the
zebra finches, for which we have not only one character but two, both
giving a somewhat similar visual coloring. The most commonly met
with is the dominant dilute which, when added to the normal gray,
produces the silver zebra finch and, to fawn, gives the cream zebra
finch.

Today we have many different mutations; this fact I feel sure caused many fanciers keen on bird breeding to take a special interest in the production of zebra finches, and in 1952 in England even a special Society for their development was founded: in our country we have "The Zebra Finch Society of America, Inc."

The paradise whydah is one of the most popular of aviary birds, and the cock in full plumage is one of the most striking of common foreign birds. It is gentle in disposition, hardy, long-lived and harmless to both plants and other birds in the aviary.

The remarkable head of a male gray zebra finch.

8. Grey/fawn-brown x fawn-brown/white gives:
12½%—grey/fawn-brown males
12½%—grey females
12½%—grey/fawn-brown/white males
12½%—grey/white females
12½%—fawn-brown males
12½%—fawn-brown females
12½%—fawn-brown/white males
12½%—fawn-brown/white females

9. Grey/white x grey gives:
25%—grey/white males
25%—grey/white females
25%—grey males
25%—grey females

Both parents share the duties of incubation, which takes twelve to fourteen days. The young leave the nest in about a fortnight and are self-supporting in another ten to twelve days. They should be separated from their parents at five weeks or they will disturb the old birds by crowding into the nest boxes. Young zebra finches resemble their mother, but have black beaks. They assume adult plumage within a few weeks.

10. Grey/white x grey/white gives:
16⅔%—grey males
16⅔%—grey females
16⅔%—grey/white males
16⅔%—grey/white females
16⅔%—white/grey males (black-eyed)
16⅔%—white/grey females (black-eyed)

11. Grey/white x fawn-brown gives:
25%—grey/fawn-brown males
25%—grey females
25%—grey/fawn-brown/white males
25%—grey/white females

12. Grey/white x fawn-brown/white gives:
16⅔%—grey/fawn-brown males
16⅔%—grey females
16⅔%—grey/fawn-brown/white males

Zebras are better able to adapt themselves to different climates than many other bird species. Nevertheless, it is as well to provide some heat during the very cold spells of weather.

16⅔%—grey/white females
16⅔%—white/grey/fawn-brown males (black-eyed)
16⅔%—white/grey females (black-eyed)

13. Grey/white x white/grey gives:
25%—grey/white males
25%—grey/white females
25%—white/grey males (black-eyed)
25%—white/grey females (black-eyed)

14. Grey/white x white/fawn-brown gives:
25%—grey/fawn-brown/white males
25%—grey/white females
25%—white/grey/fawn-brown males (black-brown-eyed)
25%—white/grey females (black-eyed)

Overcrowding during breeding operations only results in squabbling and fighting, and the stronger birds will soon develop into bullies and make life miserable for their weaker companions.

15. Grey/fawn-brown/white x grey gives:

12½%—grey males
12½%—grey females
12½%—grey/fawn-brown males
12½%—grey/white females
12½%—grey/white males
12½%—fawn-brown females
12½%—grey/fawn-brown/white males
12½%—fawn-brown/white females

16. Grey/fawn-brown/white x grey/white gives:

8⅓%—grey males
8⅓%—grey females
8⅓%—grey/fawn-brown males
8⅓%—grey/white females
8⅓%—grey/white males
8⅓%—fawn-brown females
8⅓%—grey/fawn-brown/white males
8⅓%—fawn-brown/white females
8⅓%—white/grey males (black-eyed)
8⅓%—white/grey females (black-eyed)
8⅓%—white/grey/fawn-brown males (black-brown-eyed)
8⅓%—white/fawn-brown females (red-eyed)

17. Grey/fawn-brown/white x fawn-brown gives:

12½%—grey/fawn-brown males
12½%—grey females
12½%—grey/fawn-brown/white males
12½%—grey/white females
12½%—fawn-brown males
12½%—fawn-brown females
12½%—fawn-brown/white males
12½%—fawn-brown/white females

Zebra finches often molt at irregular seasons, and it is quite useless to breed from half-molted birds. Every prospective pair of breeding birds should be in the best of health and plumage.

18. Grey/fawn-brown/white x white gives:

14 2/7%—grey/white males

14 2/7%—grey/white females

14 2/7%—grey/fawn-brown/white males

14 2/7%—white females

14 2/7%—white males

14 2/7%—fawn-brown/white females

14 2/7%—white/fawn-brown males

It has been found by experience with the zebra finch that the actual colors as well as the markings are definitely determined by more than one gene (the carriers of the heredity factors). There are elements in the various chromosomes that are in close contact with one another and working together, yet transmitting characters independently. But we need not get into complicated theory. I must admit that it does not make our task easier, for among the various elements that are joined together and work together in the different chromosomes, a very large proportion are formed in the *sex chromosomes*. The rest are formed in the normal chromosomes, also called *autosomes*. If we look again at the examples given, the results will not seem strange and may even become clear and logical. Just remember the sex-linked heredity factors and bear in mind that there are colors that are hidden or, to use the right term, split.

Finally, there is a fact worth mentioning which is complicated but very interesting. After many years of laboratory experimentation, it has been determined that the normal grey zebra finch possesses two genes for grey color which are independent and cannot exercise any influence over each other. One of these independent genes is found in a sex chromosome and the other is in an autosome.

White zebras are beautiful in their gleaming whiteness. The only other color on them is the brightly contrasting orange on beaks, feet, and legs.

The White Zebra Finch

All colors are recessive in relation to grey except silver. The white zebra finch is actually a grey bird, but it has two kinds of white factors, one with nothing more and one recessive or split for white factor. These two, acting together, "push aside" the dominant grey. When a bird has two equal recessive factors, then that color becomes visible.

I already said that, except for grey, all colors, including white, are carried recessively so that theoretically a white zebra finch could be used to produce all kinds of colors, but this would hardly make sense. Thus we know of white zebra finches that have been bred from fawn-brown and even masked zebra finches and multi-coloreds. Since fawn-brown and multi-colored are hereditarily sex-linked, if we crossed for example fawn-brown x white, we would end up with a hodge-podge of colors such as grey males split for fawn-brown and white along with fawn-brown females which are split for white.

White males have a darker shade of red-orange on their beaks and can therefore be distinguished from the females.

The heredity pattern is as follows:

1. White x white gives:
50%—white males
50%—white females

2. White x grey gives:
50%—grey/white males
50%—grey/white females

3. White x grey/white gives:
25%—white males
25%—white females
25%—grey/white females*
25%—grey/white females*

4. Grey/white x grey/white gives:
16⅔%—grey males
16⅔%—grey females
16⅔%—grey/white males
16⅔%—grey/white females
16⅔%—white/grey males (black-eyed)
16⅔%—white/grey females (black-eyed)

5. Grey/white x grey gives:
25%—grey males
25%—grey females
25%—grey/white males
25%—grey/white females

If we begin without a grey, we get:

1. Non-white x non-white naturally gives:
50%—non-white males

*Outwardly these birds look like grey zebra finches, but if they are bred
further the white will force out the grey.

There are several color varieties or mutations of zebra finches, but all are rather rare and costly in this country.

50%—non-white females

2. Non-white x white gives:
50%—split white males**
50%—split white females**

** In fawn-brown, masked or multi-colored, it is the male that is split for fawn-brown, masked or multi-colored.

3. Non-white x split white gives:
25%—non-white males
25%—non-white females
25%—split white males
25%—split white females

Color mutations are highly interesting to specialists and students of genetics.

Clear, pure white zebra finches can best be bred from *fawn-brown*. Less desirable in my opinion, but still better than breeding from normal grey or white, is cream (bred from a combination of silver x fawn-brown, about which I will speak later). Grey is less suitable as it gives us white birds with a somewhat greyish cast on the back and occasionally even on the wings and underbody. The birds look a bit grubby but, in spite of my own objections, if someone wants to make such a crossing I would not stop him. The dirty grey cast can become much less visible after several matings but does not disappear entirely. Understandably, these birds do not have a chance in a show. White zebra finches are not as strong as normal greys.

Be aware that males and females look virtually identical. Sometimes the bill of the male is a more intensely red, but this cannot be used for a sure identification. Therefore, have it understood between you and your dealer that, if after a time the birds you bought do not pair, you can exchange one of the birds.

With a little patience you will be able to tell the sexes apart. The surest distinction is the song of the male, whose full trumpeting does away with all confusion. At breeding time he behaves like a real Don Juan, flying after all the females including those of a different color if you keep them together. He busily courts them and drags in nesting material. In short, you will never have difficulty identifying the sexes during the mating season.

Zebras are often bought from advertisements. They travel well by train or air transport. They are generally sent in shallow wooden boxes, with a few holes for air, and a perch or two fixed near the floor. Seed is generally scattered on the floor.

The Gouldian finch has often been called the most beautiful bird in the world, and is a prime favorite with aviculturists, in spite of the fact that it is a tricky bird to manage. Once acclimated it is surprisingly hardy if kept at a constant temperature of about 30°C (86°F).

Albino Zebra Finches (pseudo-albino zebra finches)

It is logical at this point to follow the white zebra finches with a discussion of albino birds, although we are not talking here about breeding for color. There are few breeders who use the term "albino zebra finches" since the birds have, as you know, *red* feet and *red* bills, while real albinos lack all color or pigment, so true albino birds would have colorless feet and beaks. The eyes are red because the blood vessels are now visible since the iris of the eye is colorless. Our "pseudo-albino" zebra finches have red legs, red bills and red eyes, so we know that at least a limited amount of pigment is present; the pseudo-albino then can be thought of as a *white* zebra finch that "went wrong."

Birds with an intensely red eye color and no other coloring are true albinos. At the moment they do not exist, but with the developments taking place in the whole area of breeding and the results being achieved, it will not be long before such a bird appears on the market.

A fawn pair of zebra finches.

The two white factors (namely one white factor and one recessive or split factor) in the pseudo-albinos are supported by two other factors, fawn-brown or cream, depending naturally from which color the bird was bred. We do not have to concern ourselves about whether the pseudo-albinos are split for fawn-brown or cream. However, the recessive factors play a big role. We will get a pseudo-albino if we apply the following cross: white x fawn-brown. To avoid confusion, let me point out that a 100% white (homozygous) bird x homozygous normal grey produces a 100% split for white. You should also know that pseudo-albinos resulting from a crossing of white x cream possess the *silver factors*.

The Fawn-Brown Zebra Finch

Along with the white and grey, the fawn-brown zebra finch is among the best known, and just because it is so commonly known and has been written about so much lately, it is unfortunately called by a variety of names. In conversations with breeders and in both national and international publications, I have come across at least four different names: fawn-brown, brown, isabel and cinnamon. It is much easier when a standard name is used. There may be a slight difference between these colors, but the variations are so small as to be negligible. Far more important is the fact that all the birds of this color are of the same genetic composition. I am happy to say that over the past few years the name of fawn-brown is being used more and more, which I believe is correct.

In the grey zebra finch we find a much darker color present: a zebra finch is a *melanin* carrier, a bird that possesses black and brown pigments (the color that is in the skin). It is on record that in 1942 a South African breeder successfully did away with the black through a brown mutation. The under layer of this bird actually remains white, so the name *brown* zebra finch is not really correct.

Always keep the floor of the cage or the aviary clean and covered with sand, on which cage bird grit is sprinkled. Remove all the stale green food or soft food at the end of the day. Do not give birds wet or frosted green food.

Red-headed finches. The sexes of this species are easy to distinguish, but they are practically impossible to breed in an aviary with other birds, as they are quite easily disturbed.

From recent reports it appears that Mr. Mills definitely has bred fawn-brown zebra finches, but he certainly is not the first to do so. In May 1960 in *De Vogelgids* appeared the article "Two Little Birds Came to Warm Themselves by a Campfire. Result: the Fawn-brown Zebra Finch." The article was taken from the well known English bird magazine *Cage Birds*. With permission from the editors, I quote several excerpts.

"Had an Australian bird enthusiast not been such a keen observer while he was sojourning in South Australia, and if his brother in Adelaide had not had such good breeding results, then the fawn-brown zebra finch might well have been lost to the bird breeding world. The enthusiast who is responsible for first introducing the fawn-colored variety is Mr. M. Lewitzka. When he lived in Coward Springs, about 500 miles north of Adelaide, he observed and caught the birds that finally produced the fawn color. It was his

A suitable cage for one pair of zebra finches.

brother, F. Lewitzka, who attempted to create a new stock and finally culminated his efforts with the production of the fawn-colored zebra finches such as we see every day. Both men have done much in the interest of the bird breeding hobby. The fawn-colored zebra finches were first introduced in 1927."

The writer goes on to say that the original birds were encountered in dry, sparsely vegetated country in terrain that lies outside the normal rainfall area. During the day it is terribly hot, but the evenings are so cold that people travelling through always have to build camp fires. In this region, among a large flock of normal greys, two fawn-colored zebra finches flew down to warm themselves a bit by the dying

209

embers. The two birds were successfully caught. According to the description, it seems that their color was just like that of our present breeding birds. Both birds, females, were immediately taken to Adelaide. The breeder began to breed the birds with the hope of getting offspring exactly like the females. It quickly became apparent that he was getting females with all sorts of color deviations, but none which were fawn-colored. They were a "poor copy of our present day silver-colored birds. They were spotty and certainly did not make a good impression." The first males that were bred were conspicuous for the small amount of color in their cheek spots. With tight-lipped determination, Mr. Lewitzka bred the same birds and quickly built up a small colony. Naturally a number of the birds were distributed to other breeders and, with their combined efforts, they finally succeeded in breeding the first fawn-colored zebra finch. Soon after, this mutation was firmly established.

"When," continues the article, "the fawn color became available in sizeable quantity, the fundamental principles were soon neglected and the birds were bred in a free-for-all manner. As a result, there appeared other mutations which the breeders used with an eye to developing new varieties. While some breeders with less ability lost ground, others were lucky enough to progress further until all the mutations were firmly established, many of which showed up quite unexpectedly." It is quite possible that Mr. F. Mills from Johannesburg in 1942 bred the pure fawn-brown zebra finch and once again definitely set the ball rolling in the right direction.

At the moment there are a good number of fawn-brown zebra finches being bred which have very small deviations that do not show. They must appear light brown to darker brown. In general, the lighter browns are rated higher by the judges than the darker ones. As a general rule, *always pair the lightest colors with each other*. If it is ever necessary to have a fawn-brown zebra finch that stands up on all points, the

A female St. Helena waxbill from Central Africa feeding a young male.

lightness of color is important. If the bird is also in good condition and has good form, you may well have a prize-winner.

Light birds are those which possess the white factor; dark zebra finches do not have it. Perhaps it would be best to call these birds by the names single-factored fawn-brown zebra finch and double-factored fawn-brown zebra finch. A crossing between both colors (remember that we are dealing with a mutant bird) gives more or less of a hodgepodge. The colors stay somewhere between light and dark, but there can be quite light birds and quite dark birds among them as well. You can see that this manner of breeding simply relies on coincidence and should be most emphatically discouraged.

Violet-eared waxbills. Unfortunately, this lovely waxbill is rather difficult to keep and will not survive in a temperature below fifty
degrees. This bird is very insectivorous and is also fond of grass
seeds.

The heredity here is sex-linked. Brown females get their
color only from the brown male (their father). Here is a constant rule you would do well to keep in mind: *females can
never be split for fawn-brown, chestnut-flanked white or cream;
males, on the other hand, can be!* There exist for the females,
then, only two possibilities: either they are fawn-brown,
chestnut-flanked white or cream, or they are not. That seems
pretty simple. The heredity laws for the fawn-brown zebra
finch are as follows:

1. Fawn-brown x fawn-brown gives:
50%—fawn-brown males
50%—fawn-brown females

2. Fawn-brown x normal grey gives:
50%—grey/fawn-brown males
50%—fawn-brown females

3. Normal grey x fawn-brown gives:
50%—grey/fawn-brown males
50%—grey females

4. Grey/fawn-brown x fawn-brown gives:
25%—grey/fawn-brown males
25%—fawn-brown males
25%—grey females
25%—fawn-brown females

5. Grey/fawn-brown x grey gives:
25%—grey/fawn-brown males
25%—grey males
25%—fawn-brown females
25%—grey females

Peter's twinspot. This magnificent finch frequents dense bush and thorn tangles on river banks and spends most of its time on the ground among thick undergrowth. It is rarely on the market but is an excellent aviary bird, of hardy constitution.

Naturally these results are only obtained when we deal with 100 birds equally divided between males and females; we are speaking theoretically. In practice, the final result of a single crossing can give rather different percentages, especially when we know for certain that a normal clutch of eggs consists of an uneven number of eggs: three to seven. Over the course of time, the combined offspring of a pair will indeed agree with the theoretical results.

Because the fawn-brown is such a favorite of those breeding for color, I am giving a table similar to the one for normal grey zebra finches. From this list you will see that the rules I have given above are constant.

1. Fawn-brown x fawn-Brown gives:
50%—fawn-brown males
50%—fawn-brown females

2. Fawn-brown x white/fawn-brown gives:
50%—fawn-brown/white males
50%—fawn-brown/white females

3. Fawn-brown/white x normal grey gives:
25%—grey/fawn-brown males
25%—fawn-brown females
25%—fawn-brown/ white females
25%—grey/fawn-brown/white males

4. Fawn-brown x normal grey gives:
50%—grey/fawn-brown males
50%—fawn-brown females

5. Fawn-brown x grey/white gives:
25%—grey/fawn-brown males
25%—fawn-brown females
25%—grey/fawn-brown/white males
25%—fawn-brown/white females

6. Fawn-brown/white x grey/white gives:
16⅔%—grey/fawn-brown males
16⅔%—fawn-brown females
16⅔%—grey/fawn-brown/white males
16⅔%—fawn-brown/white females
16⅔%—white/grey/fawn-brown males
16⅔%—white/fawn-brown females

7. Fawn-brown/white x fawn-brown gives:
25%—fawn-brown males
25%—fawn-brown females
25%—fawn-brown/white males
25%—fawn-brown/white females

8. Fawn-brown/white x fawn-brown/white gives:
16⅔%—fawn-brown males
16⅔%—fawn-brown females
16⅔%—fawn-brown/white males

White eyes or Zosterops are sometimes called spectacle birds, and in Australia they are called silver eyes. Most of the eighty-five species reaching aviculture come from India, Japan or Hong Kong. The birds are very hardy and easy to feed. They eat the standard nectar food plus fruit, sponge cake, peanut butter, live food and mynah meal.

Many birds relish some live food each day and require it during the breeding season. Here is one way of catching insects and such!

16⅔%—fawn-brown/white females
16⅔%—white/fawn-brown males
16⅔%—white/fawn-brown females

9. Fawn brown/white x grey/white gives:
25%—grey/fawn-brown/white males
25%—fawn-brown/white females
25%—white/grey/fawn-brown males
25%—white/fawn-brown females

10. Fawn-brown/white x white/fawn brown gives:
25%—fawn-brown/white males
25%—fawn-brown males
25%—white/fawn-brown males
25%—white/fawn-brown females

These charts tell us a few things. First is the fact that fawn-brown is a sex-related heredity factor. To have good stock to breed, the breeder would do best to start by buying a pure-bred (homozygous) couple or, to save money and enjoy doing the breeding yourself, buy a pure-bred *male* which is well marked, light in color and of strong structure. With the first crossing the male is paired with a pure-bred female. By crossing the father back we get pure-bred females and males. Here again is an example of advantageous in-breeding

Further on in the charts, we see that there are crossings which give us, in one nest, grey and grey/fawn-brown males. It would be best to avoid these because, in spite of their similar outward appearance, only a small percentage of the birds are heterozygous.

I want to point out again that all recessive colors in fawn-brown can be bred. Also remember that white is recessive to all colors.

A. Rutgers makes an interesting observation about the fawn-brown zebra finch: "From the crossing of the sex-linked fawn-brown color with birds carrying silver dominant, we get what should be called silver-brown but what is generally called cream. Here the double factor will not appear because the double factored silver is presumed to be lethal. You will find that you cannot breed homozygotic cream birds because the fawn-brown color will continue to show up."

The Silver Zebra Finch

The silver zebra finch is also often called "pastel blue" or "blue," but these names are wrong. It is very important to know that the *silver* factor is the only one that is dominant over grey. It can appear as a single (= split for grey) or as a double (silver-silver). Other than that, the birds cannot be distinguished from one another. Most silvers are single-factored, so it is difficult to speak of possible color differences. In judging circles, they prefer to say that the silver factor is a bleaching factor, which means that through the silver factor the normal grey becomes less intense. Because of the fact that the silver factor is visible, there can be no question of a split. This holds true even though the white zebra finch possesses a split or hidden silver factor which can not be seen *outwardly*. We know of no grey zebra finches that are split for silver. Grey x (recessive) white gives 100% grey/white; silver x (recessive) grey gives 50% grey and 50% silver/grey. The bird keeper can draw the logical conclusion that, by in-breeding the last example, silver/grey x silver/grey, offspring will come forth which are double-factored silver (according to the figures, it will be 25%; moreover, 25% grey and 50% single-factored silver split for grey). But according to Rutgers this does not work: "We do not find the double factors; all silvers that we get are heterozygotic and therefore split again in grey and silver; grey is worthless in breeding silver because it does not possess that factor."

About the meaning of "single" and "double" I will make a few remarks. A silver zebra finch with the single factor is generally a bit paler than the one with the double factor. The difference need not always be visible, for we know that there are other factors that cause differences from one zebra finch to another. The influence is there, and they come up against one another. Sometimes the silver zebra finch is difficult to recognize, and there are times when some grey and fawn-browns are difficult to distinguish from silver. Consequently, it is important that we can theoretically go back and see if there isn't a silver factor in play here. And we must not forget that both sexes of the silver zebra finch do have the possibility (or at least can have the possibility) of transmitting white. Along with this is the possibility that the males can transmit fawn-brown. The rule then is: silver (single or double) appears first if either the male or the female is silver.

We can arrive at the following heredity rules (SS is the

double factor and S the single factor):

1. SS-silver x SS-silver gives:
100%—SS-silver

2. SS-silver x S-silver gives:
50%—SS-silver
50%—S-silver

3. S-silver x S-silver gives:
25%—SS-silver
25%—normal grey
50%—S-silver

4. SS-silver x normal grey gives:
100%—S-silver

5. S-silver x normal grey gives:
50%—S-silver
50%—normal grey

Silvers are often paired with normal greys to improve the size and type, because the normal grey is still superior in these respects. A normal grey cannot be split for silver; the very doubtful recessive silver is only a remote possibility. The contention that silver can be bred by intensively breeding white x normal grey is based on a misunderstanding; there is no possibility of getting silver.

The Cream Zebra Finch
The cream or brown-silver zebra finch appears when we cross a homozygous silver with a homozygous fawn-brown. By this crossing two characters show up, namely the sex-linked fawn-brown and the dominant silver.

In order to get the desired result as quickly as possible, you should pair a fawn-brown male with a silver female, which will give you silver males split for fawn-brown and single-factored silver-brown females. When we pair these last females with silver males split for fawn-brown, then we get cream females and silver isabel males. If the silver isabel male is then paired with a cream female, we get cream males split for silver isabel or fawn-brown. It is a pity that we do not get enough pure-breds. A cream zebra finch with one silver factor is never as clear in color as a bird with a double silver factor. The cream birds also carry a white factor which becomes very apparent in double-factored birds.

From the previous paragraph we know that we have double- and single-factored silver zebra finches, that is, with SS or S, which brings us to the following heredity table:

1. Fawn-brown male x SS-silver female gives:
50%—S-silver males, split for fawn-brown
50%—S-silver cream females

2. Fawn-brown male x S-silver female gives:
25%—grey, split for fawn-brown males
25%—S-silver, split for fawn-brown males
25%—fawn-brown females
25%—S-silver cream females

3. SS-silver male x fawn-brown female gives:
50%—S-silver males, split for fawn-brown
50%—S-silver females

This does not give us cream; cream appears first when we pair a silver male split for fawn-brown with a fawn-brown female. This results in:

MALES
25%—cream
25%—grey/fawn-brown
220

25%—fawn-brown
25%—silver

FEMALES
25%—cream
25%—grey
25%—fawn-brown
25%—silver

We get the most beautiful birds by crossing very light fawn-browns with very light silvers.

King's or pintailed whydah. Males, when in their ornamental plumage, are rather aggressive and can frighten other birds in the aviary. Given sufficient room, they can be kept together with weavers and zebra finches.

Multi-Colored or Variegated Zebra Finches

White bred to grey does not give a multi-colored mutation. We must be particularly careful that the more-or-less clear white flecks and stripes in the coat of feathers are evenly spaced. This is quite a feat, but if we want to breed well-marked and well-colored stock we must use parents as nearly identical as possible. Otherwise we will end up with a motley assortment of markings. As you know, multi-colored is recessive to grey. We can establish this in the following chart:

1. Multi-colored x multi-colored gives:
100%—multi-colored males and females

2. Multi-colored x pure-bred grey gives:
100%—grey, split for multi-colored

3. Multi-colored x grey gives:
50%—grey, split for multi-colored (normal/multi-colored)
50%—multi-colored

With the multi-colored recessive to grey, we cross a multi-color male x white female and get multi-colored offspring (50%) and grey offspring split for multi-colored (50%). So again, we have bred grey birds!

Keep in mind that multi-color is a mutation. Experience has shown that a multi-color factor is present in grey. Furthermore, it must be said that there are unfortunately some dreadful multi-colored zebra finches. Although we can breed multi-coloreds in all colors, the best results are gotten with grey (naturally) and to a lesser degree fawn-brown.

Because multi-color is in fact difficult to maintain, it seems most sensible to follow this rule: if you have bred multi-color once with different couples, then always pair multi-color x multi-color. Now, it may happen that sooner or later you will find it necessary to resort to in-breeding. If you find after a time that the birds are regressing in color, size and shape, then cross again with grey (or fawn-brown).

Chestnut-Flanked White Zebra Finch

The chestnut-flanked white male, also called "masked," is completely creamy white. The eye stripe is kept but is of a lighter color, as are the somewhat smaller breast markings. The male also has cheek and side markings which are less pronounced than, for example, in the normal grey. It is far

A pair of Dufresne's waxbills from South Africa. This delightful little waxbill has been fairly frequently imported in the past, but is always rather expensive. Unfortunately it is not hardy and should be wintered in a warm place. It is also rather short-lived.

from easy and demands considerable skill to retain the white and silver white in the coat of feathers. The chestnut-flanked white female is essentially totally white though in most cases the eye stripes are still present.

Here again we are dealing with sex-related heredity. The heredity rules are as follows:

1. Chestnut-flanked white x chestnut-flanked white gives:
100%—chestnut-flanked white (males and females)

2. Chestnut-flanked white x non chestnut-flanked white gives:
50%—split for masked (males)
50%—pure chestnut-flanked white (females)

3. Split masked x chestnut-flanked white (you see that either name can be used) gives:
25%—split for masked (males)
25%—pure chestnut-flanked white (males)
25%—non chestnut-flanked white (females)
25%—homozygous masked (females)

4. Non chestnut-flanked white x homozygous chestnut-flanked white gives:
50%—split for chestnut-flanked white (males)
50%—non chestnut-flanked white (females)

5. Split for chestnut-flanked white x non chestnut-flanked white gives:
25%—split for chestnut-flanked white (males)
25%—non chestnut-flanked (males)
25%—chestnut-flanked (females)
25%—non chestnut-flanked (females)
(This last crossing is not recommended.)

Since the "masked" color is hereditarily sex-linked, we know chestnut-flanked white females are not split for certain colors. Therefore, if you want to start with this color, begin with a chestnut-flanked white *male*, not a chestnut-flanked white female.

When we cross a normal grey male x chestnut-flanked white female, we get males that are split for chestnut-flanked white (or masked). The females from such a crossing are of

224

course not chestnut-flanked white. If we use a pure-bred (homozygous) chestnut-flanked white male and a pure-bred grey female, the result will be that both sexes will be chestnut-flanked white or masked. Naturally, only the males can be split. These males transmit a good, solid chestnut-flanked white.

Red-headed finch. This species resembles the cut-throat finch but differs in the distribution of its pattern of markings; it also is a bigger bird.

White Throated Zebra Finch or Silverwing

These birds, recessive in relation to grey, are also known as "penguin" zebra finches. The belly, breast and throat are clear white, while the back and wings are dark grey. This description comes from the colors one encountered in the 1930's. You may come across other names given to the silverwing. The birds are certainly not uniform. I have seen, for example, light grey, clear silver grey, silver grey, dark and light isabel, cream and a variety of intermediate colors.

The silverwing must never have the well known zebra finch markings. The correct colors are white breast and belly, white cheeks, as far as possible a white tail, and no markings on the breast and throat; the grey of the wings, head and back should be a silver grey, and the eyes should be black. We must use correctly colored and marked birds for pairing otherwise we rule out the serious, meticulous breeding that gives us the opportunity to eventually achieve new color combinations by crossing the silverwing with other colors. We lose all control when we accept all colors that look something like the white throat and may even be called by that name. I feel that the best crossing is a light grey male (grey with a touch of white) x grey female (grey with no white cast). The male has no zebra markings.

You may well say: "All well and good, but if I have birds which do have some breast stripes and the head markings are not exactly right, there isn't much else I can do about it than use these birds for breeding."

You can of course breed with the birds you have. It will just take longer before you get pure silverwings. Always keep as your goal the loss of the breast markings on the male. This is one of the smallest demands made by exhibition judges. Standards are now international, so if you ever intend to sell your birds in other countries you must give considerable consideration to good form and color.

For a second pairing we can take a silverwing male with a minimum of white cast on its wings and pair him with a lighter female (with a touch of white). Both birds showed should be homozygous and of good form and color.

Silverwing is transmitted as a recessive trait. The heredity rules are as follows:

1. Silverwing x silverwing gives:
100%—silverwing, males as well as females

2. Non-silverwing x silverwing gives:
100%—split for silverwing

3. Split for silverwing x silverwing gives:
50%—homozygous silverwing
50%—split for silverwing

The cut-throat or ribbon finch. The hen lacks the red throat band and the chocolate abdomen. She is very susceptible to egg-binding in cold weather, and this is the one snag in building up a stock of these birds.

Melba finches have been bred regularly in Europe and Australia for some years, the young being reared on supplies of termites or 'white ants.' Some pairs have proved ready breeders, whereas others, apparently just as fit, refuse to nest.

4. Split for silverwing x split for silverwing gives:
25%—split for silverwing
25%—homozygous silverwing
50%—non-silverwing

A more difficult crossing to make is one between a bird that is split for silverwing by one that is not a silverwing. The offspring are not distinguishable from one another. If we know for certain that the male is split for silverwing and the female is not a silverwing, the result is 50% split for silverwing and 50% that are not silverwings.

228

Other Zebra Finch Colors

Normal brown zebra finch
This color is sex-linked.

1. Grey x normal brown gives:
grey-brown males and grey females

2. Grey/brown x brown gives:
25% brown males
25% grey/brown males
25% brown females
25% grey females

3. Brown x grey gives:
grey-brown males
brown females

Black-crested finch or crested bunting, formerly called pigmy cardinals. This is a very attractively patterned finch of medium size.

4. Brown x blackback (paleback) gives:
grey/brown and blackback males and brown females (crossing over!)

5. Blackback x brown gives:
grey/brown and blackback males and blackback females (crossing over!)

6. Brown x blackmask gives:
grey/brown and blackmask males and blackmask females (crossing over!)

Blackmask zebra finch
This color is sex-linked.

1. Mask x blackback gives:
blackback/mask males
mask females

2. Blackback/mask x mask gives:
25% mask males
25% blackback/mask males
25% blackback females
25% mask females
Do not use other colors as this will harm the blackmask color mutation.

Blackback or paleback zebra finches
This color is sex-linked. It is a mutation of the same gene as the blackmask, therefore it is easy to get quite a few palebacks via blackmasks. The best crossings are:

1. Blackback x mask gives:
blackback/mask males
blackback females

2. Blackback/mask x mask gives:
25% blackback/mask males
25% mask males
25% blackback females
25% mask females

3. Grey x blackback gives:
grey/blackback males
grey females

4. Blackback x grey gives:
grey/blackback males
blackback females

5. Grey/blackback x blackback gives:
25% grey/blackback males
25% blackback males
25% grey females
25% blackback females

Red-billed weavers. This frequently imported, industrious African bird will begin construction of a nest almost immediately upon placement in an aviary. They are always busy and will often destroy one nest in order to start another. They are colony nesters.

As proof that both mutations (blackback and blackmask) are of the same gene, note the following crossing:

6. Grey/blackback x mask gives:
25% grey/mask males
25% blackback/mask males
25% grey females
25% blackback females
If we were dealing with *two* mutations then the result would be:

Grey/blackback x mask gives:
25% grey/mask males
25% grey/blackback and mask males
25% grey females
25% blackback females
All the males would be *grey*, even with a crossing blackback x mask!

Silver-blue tanager *(Thraupis virens)*. This species, from Central and South America, is a hardy bird once acclimated; it is inclined to be spiteful with smaller birds.

Blackbreast zebra finch
This mutation comes from Germany (1970) and is still extremely rare.

1. Blackbreast x normal grey gives:
100% grey/blackbreast (males and females)

2. Grey/blackbreast x blackbreast gives:
50% grey/blackbreast (males and females)
50% blackbreast (males and females)

The same applies for normal grey x blackbreast and blackbreast x grey/blackbreast.

3. Grey blackbreast x brown gives:
grey/blackbreast and brown males
grey/blackbreast females

4. Brown x grey blackbreast gives:
grey/blackbreast + brown males
brown/blackbreast females

5. Grey/blackbreast + brown x brown/blackbreast gives:
grey blackbreast/brown males
grey/blackbreast + brown males
brown/blackbreast males
brown blackbreast males
grey/brown males
brown males
grey blackbreast females
brown/blackbreast females
brown blackbreast females
grey females
brown females

Greywing zebra finch

1. Grey x greywing and greywing x grey gives:
grey/greywing for both males and females

2. Grey/greywing x grey/greywing gives:
25% greywing
25% grey
50% grey/greywing

3. Grey/greywing x greywing gives:
50% greywing
50% grey/greywing

Brownwing zebra finch
This color comes from breeding two mutations: brown and greywing.

1. Greywing x brown gives:
grey/greywing males
brown and grey/greywing females

2. Brown x greywing gives:
grey/greywing and brown males
brown/brownwing females

Frontal view of a 'dual-sexed' zebra finch; one side of the bird is the "male-marked" side, the other the "female-marked" side.

Black-headed mannikin. This is one of the most popular of foreign finches. It is a good bird for the beginner, being hardy and pretty in a quiet way. Its efforts at singing are very amusing; after much gesticulation the cock emits a faint squeak exactly like the mew of a kitten heard from a distance.

3. Grey/greywing and brown x brown/brownwing gives:
grey/brown males
grey brown and brownwing males
brown males
brown/brownwing males
greywing/brownwing males
brownwing males
grey females
grey/greywing females
greywing females
brown females
brown/brownwing females
brownwing females

Crested or tufted zebra finch

This is a dominant mutation. The double factor is lethal. Therefore the crossing crested x non-crested is by far the best. A crossing like crested x non-crested gives 50% crested females and males.

St. Helena waxbill. Like the other waxbills, this species will use a covered nest box or construct a spherical nest in a bush. The nest is made of interwoven grasses and has a bottle-neck side entrance. Feathers are used in quantity as a lining. The birds do not like any interference with their nest and will desert rather readily.

Chapter 4. New
Breeding Possibilities

One of the new possibilities is the blue zebra finch, which has been described in detail by Stork. He contends that the bird is a breeding product of actually nothing other than a silver, and I believe he is correct. This we know: the heredity factor is dominant, and these birds cannot be distinguished from the true pure-colored silvers. Some of the so-called blue zebra finches we come across have some fawn-brown or cream in the wings and tails. We need not bother ourselves with this now, for I believe it will be a few years before it is firmly established whether or not we are dealing with a new color. I will make this request of my readers: if there is among you anyone who is firmly convinced that a blue zebra finch really exists, would he please let me know by contacting the publisher. At the moment there is nothing more that can be said about this color. Time will tell us if the blue zebra finch will show up as a new breed just as did, for example, the albino and cream zebra finches, which we know are mutations. The same holds true for other colors that we see sporadically at exhibitions or come across in shops occasionally.

I said in the beginning of this book that we are just at the starting point in the art and practice of breeding zebra finches for color. For example, it seems quite impossible to me to be able to breed a red zebra finch. In order to get a red coat of feathers, we must have at our disposal an unfamiliar tropical bird that, to the best of my knowledge has never been available in our land, namely, *Haematospiza sipahi*, called the Sepoy finch by the English. This little bird comes from somewhere in the Himalayas. The male is almost totally red with a few shiny brownish grey feathers along the wings and sides. The possibility of breeding a black zebra finch is not out of the question, and it should also be possible to breed pure albinos.

As soon as breeders know more about the combined effects of heredity factors, they will undoubtedly breed a greater variety of colors and even forms. It is almost unthinkable, but there is always the danger that these possibilities may affect the intrinsic characters of the zebra finch—his quick little eye and the typical markings on its breast and sides that gave it its name. But I can see how the ideas that have been mentioned can spark the imagination.

Male Cordon Bleu *(Uraeginthus bengalus)*. This species will breed when about six months old, and it is their natural inclination to breed all the year round. But this can only be allowed by fanciers living in warm countries; those in northern climes must discourage the breeding of these birds except in warm summer weather, otherwise hens will almost certainly succumb to egg-binding.

Red-eared waxbills. This species is most commonly imported, and though an active little bird and fairly hardy as an aviary inmate, it has been bred on only a few occasions. It not infrequently builds a nest and lays eggs, but it rarely progresses any further.

Finally, I will discuss another possibility, the breeding of zebra finches with *hybrids,* which is the crossing of a zebra finch with another kind of bird. The breeding of these "bastards" has, from the viewpoint of the bird expert, the obvious disadvantage that one can never get a racially pure bird. On the other hand, the bird keeper can well open up a fascinating new world of color and form by using hybrids.

Up to now the best known crossing possibilities (both sexes can be crossed) with zebra finches are:

Bichenow's finch, masked grass finch, star finch, long-tailed grass finch, chestnut-breasted finch, St. Helena wax-bill, cherry finch, fire finch, diamond sparrow, African silver-bill, black-ringed finch, black-headed mannikin, Bengalese or society finch, and three-colored mannikin.

239

Avadavat or tiger finch. This species differs from all other waxbills in having a seasonal change of plumage, normally being out of color from December until March. It is a first-rate cage and aviary bird and a fairly free breeder. It likes to line its nest with feathers, cotton-wool, down, etc. When courting, the cock dances around the hen with head erect, crown feathers raised, tail spread like a fan, and uttering his pleasant little song.

III. OTHER SMALL EXOTIC BIRDS

Since zebra finches are not bellicose, it is quite easy to house them with other birds. Obviously their "companions" should be calm and restful during and out of the brooding season.

Avadavat or tiger finch *(Amandava amandava)*
The avadavat is a charming little bird from Indonesia and India that is well known and popular among bird keepers. The colorful male with its red coat and (during the breeding season) numerous white spots delights the eye. The female also has the white dots. All year long the song of the male comes through with a clear tone. The female also can be heard to sing, particularly when she has no mate, but her song is less ebullient. During the breeding season the pair is enjoyable to watch. In their interesting mating dance the male, bursting into full song, spreads his tail feathers and dances around the female. The gratifying results one can get with a good couple make these birds very suitable for breeding. The necessary nesting materials are fibers, moss, blades of grass, some thin twigs and a little wool. If these are available it will not be long before the avadavats begin to build their pouch-shaped nest, preferably in a thicket. Four to seven eggs are laid, and only the female broods them while the male stays in very close to the nest and waits. The couple must not be disturbed during the breeding time or everything can go wrong. After approximately 12 days the young appear. They should be provided with a sensible seed diet—Senegal millet, canary seed, etc., plus feedings of ant eggs.

Fire finch *(Lagonosticta senegala)*

The fire finch, originally from the western part of Africa, is a rather shy bird which prefers to stay on the ground. The red male, with his constantly moving tail, is a funny little animal. The female is brown above and, like the male, has white dots on the breast. In the aviary these birds are rather withdrawn, sticking with each other and having nothing to do with other inhabitants. Many of them are brought into the shops and can be bought practically throughout the year. The birds that have just been brought in generally have a poor coat of feathers. They must be most carefully acclimated, but, since this is quite difficult to do, my advice is that you buy only those birds that have been bred in our country. Birds that are not yet acclimated find it difficult to tolerate drafts and cold. They fare best at an even temperature of 18°-20 °C.

In closed nest boxes they build a "cradle" from the same materials as the avadavats; rarely, they will make a free nest in the bushes. When we hang a nesting box in a little thicket, the birds will accept it sooner than a nesting box hung up against one of the walls of the aviary. The female broods the three or four white eggs for about 11 days. When the offspring are hatched, an extra amount of feed should be provided. Give them universal food, a good variety of egg mixture, ant eggs, egg yolk, finely cut mealworms, white worms, greens (lettuce, endive, chicory, chickweed and such) and cuttlebone. The ant eggs (pupae) can be given fresh as well as in the dry form. This is indispensable, particularly during the mating and breeding season.

Golden-breasted waxbill *(Amandava subflava)*

Another easy to keep bird is the richly colored golden-breasted waxbill from the western part of Africa. It can stay in an outside aviary during the summer but, like the avadavat and fire finch, it must spend the winter in a warmer area (around 15 °C). The golden-breasted waxbill does not

The three-colored mannikin. This species is confined to central and southern India and is not so common on the market as other *Lonchura* species.

Bengalese finches will build their nests from various materials, usually in a wooden nest box, preferably completely enclosed with only a small entrance hole at the front.

yet feel at home in our land, and the brooding results are negative, which is a pity because the beautiful birds are so decorative in the aviary. In their bulky nest a few eggs are sometimes laid, but unfortunately these are generally unfertilized. If after about a dozen days of brooding it does occur that the eggs develop, then feed the birds as you would the fire finch. During the brooding season these birds may be quarrelsome with the other birds, but if the aviary is not too densely populated and there is enough plant life to provide hiding places for those birds that want it, there should be no difficulty.

Green singing finch. This delightful little finch is really more yellow than green. The sexes are rather alike, though it is not really difficult to select a pair when comparing adult birds, the cock usually being of a brighter yellow while the female has a necklace of black spots across the throat. But this distinction only holds good in birds of the same age, as an old hen would be just as brightly colored as a young cock. The cock, of course, betrays his sex by singing.

Lavender finch *(Estrilda caerulescens)*

This bird, also from West Africa, is worthy of mention. The male, with his beautiful clear red color and constantly moving tail, busily sings away. The female is a bit smaller than her mate. They are peaceful birds and quite quickly become tame enough to eat from the hand of their keeper. They are real acrobats and are amusing to watch. They breed well and regularly, particularly if there are no other birds of the same variety in the same aviary. In order to build their nests, they need a large amount of material like the zebra finch. During the winter these beautiful little birds must be kept in a warm area. Feed as you would fire finches.

African silver-bill *(Euodice malabarica cantans)*

A very rewarding and frequently-found bird from South Africa. With its simple brown coat of feathers, it is a very dear and unspectacular bird that is known for its ease of breeding. In its pattern of living it is somewhat like the Bengalese, which also adopts eggs from other birds. It is difficult to get a pair because the male and female look alike. Only the song of the male can help us tell the sexes apart. It makes good sense to buy several birds; different couples get on well with each other in the same aviary. They begin to breed quickly as long as they are undisturbed during their busy brooding time. Give them the following nesting materials: fine grass, wool, horse hair and other fine material. After 12 days the young hatch and are fed by the parents for about 20 days. A clutch consists of four or five eggs; in the breeding season four clutches are not unusual.

Hen cordon bleus may be distinguished by the absence of the red ear-patch. These charming and beautiful little waxbills are great favorites with fanciers, being lively little birds, good mixers in the aviary and fairly free breeders.

Two male cordon bleus. The diet for breeding pairs must contain insect food. Cordons are very fond of the aphids that collect on beans, roses, and other plants in the summer. They will also pick up minute insects from newly turned soil.

St. Helena waxbill *(Estrilda astrild)*

This bird comes from Central Africa. It does not cope too well with cold weather but, because of its color and conscientious breeding, is much sought after. Once these birds get used to their feed (see the fire finch) their breeding results will be good. Both the male and the female take turns brooding the three or four white eggs which hatch in about 11 days. The young leave the nest after two weeks or so, but continue to be fed by the parents for a short while longer. They require fresh bath water at room temperature daily.

Indian silver-bill *(Euodice malabarica malabarica)*

The Indian silver-bill is closely related to the African silver-bill, but it comes from India. The only difference lies in the color of the top tail-covert feathers, which are white with a black border. They have other qualities in common also. They are friendly, good to keep and excellent breeders. Both sexes are identical except that the male can be distinguished by its soft song. But there are some striking differences between the two species. The Indian silver-bill lays a larger number of eggs than the African silver-bill; sometimes a clutch can consist of four to eight eggs or even ten. The larger clutches must be due to the number of couples that brood in the same nest. In the wild, I have found nests with from 20 to 25 eggs, and three times I found a "nursery" with 28(!) young ones that were just about ready to fly. It was apparent that these families came from three or four couples. In the wild they rarely build a nest but rather lay a sheathing on top of structures built by weavers. Once I found young Indian silver-bills in the nest of a white-headed mannikin.

Indian silver-bills are so closely related to African silver-bills that they can be crossed very easily. Their care and the method of feeding them is the same as for the African silver-bill. Feed like fire finches.

Spice finch *(Lonchura punctulata)*

This little 10cm-long bird from southeast Asia is lovely and easy to keep. It can be bought almost anywhere very cheaply. These birds are well known for their appealing nature and the modest demands they make upon the bird keeper. In aviaries as well as in glass enclosures these birds thrive and breed. The male sings a song we cannot hear, but by the proud thrust of its head we can see that he is busily engrossed in what he is doing. Spice finches are almost always in motion. In the winter they can be brought inside to a frost-free area, but this does not imply that they cannot

Pearl-headed silverbills. Determination of sex in these birds is difficult at best. The breast of the female is slightly lighter than that of the male and the spots slightly smaller. A more effective method is the study of the nuptial dance of the male, but even this is not always 100% effective.

tolerate our climate. Experience has shown that if they are given an outside aviary with a sturdily built night enclosure containing felt-lined nesting boxes (which also serve as sleeping places) they can spend the winter outdoors. During the day they sometimes amuse themselves in the snow, rolling and pecking around to their hearts' content. We do not recommend that the beginning bird keeper let the birds stay outside during the cold months, however. Once you have chosen a couple, you are then faced with the tough job of finding out if you have a male and female for breeding, because the sexes cannot be told apart. This is also true for the following four species.

White-headed mannikin *(Lonchura maja)*

This bird is easy to keep and strong. In India and the Sunda Islands enormous flocks are sometimes seen that can cause untold damage to crops. But in their own land as well as ours they are very much in demand. Although the breeding results from these birds are nothing to rave about, there is a small chance that a couple will breed if the cage is in a very quiet and restful spot. There is a better chance of breeding if a male white-headed mannikin is mated with a Bengalese. Once they start breeding, you can expect the young in 12 days; after 25 days or so they leave the nest but still take food from the parents for a while. Their nails grow quite long and should be carefully trimmed twice a year, a job that is far from easy but necessary. The white-headed mannikin must have fresh bath water.

Three-color mannikin *(Lonchura malacca)*
This bird comes from India and is controlled by import regulations. It is extremely strong and lively and excellent for the beginning bird keeper. These birds are fed the same food as the fire finch and are cared for in the same manner as the spice finch.

Black-headed mannikin *(Lonchura malacca atricapella)*
Along with the zebra finch, parakeet, canary and diamond pigeon, this is one of the most popular birds found in aviaries. They are very good for beginners, but it must be said that they practically never breed. There has been some success in crossing them with Bengalese, white-headed mannikins and spice finches. They are pleasant, tolerant birds that never get into arguments and bear up quite well in most circumstances. They also need fresh bath water daily and nail care. The black-headed mannikin is indeed a decorative bird that is most gratifying to keep in an indoor cage.

Magpie mannikin *(Spermestes fringilloides)*
This bird has recently become available in the shops. It comes from West and South Africa. Generally it breeds well and, although the sexes at first seem identical, you will

develop the knack of finding a pair. The male sings at great length, but his song is soft. During the breeding season the male goes through his mating dance. Magpie mannikin couples, like zebra finches, should be kept in a roomy aviary or they become restless, somewhat belligerent and generally unmanageable. These birds prefer a cage in which they can go their own way undisturbed. They lay a clutch of four to six eggs which are brooded by both sexes for 11 or 12 days. Magpie mannikins are rather undemanding birds and are quite good for the interested beginner. Feed them like fire finches.

Grey waxbill *(Estrilda troglodytes)*

Grey waxbills, also called coralbeaks, are brought in by the hundreds from Central Africa. They are funny little birds that quickly make themselves at home in glass enclosures, room aviaries and even in large outside aviaries. They are always on the go, giving out a shrill little song that is not particularly pretty but nonetheless has a certain charm. Out of the brooding season the sexes are difficult to tell apart, but this changes when the breeding time starts. The color of the male becomes a much more intense red and his eyebrows become darker. He then goes through his display, holding a blade of grass or some such thing in his beak and dancing in circles around the female while she looks on disinterestedly. But at a given moment she begins to answer the clear song of her intended mate with clucking call-notes and tender warbling. In the breeding season everything must be calm and peaceful, for these birds become very nervous and with the slightest disturbance may desert the eggs or the young. Their bullet-shaped nests should be built in a hidden area of the aviary—a closed nesting box, for example. Three to five eggs are laid and then brooded alternately by the male and female, generally for periods of three hours each. After 11 or 12 days the eggs hatch. The young leave the nest after two weeks but, like many of the other birds, continue to take food from the parents for a while longer. These birds generally breed two or three times a year provided the aviary is peaceful. After the last brooding, grey waxbills begin to molt and it is then advisable to bring them into an evenly warmed place. They must be kept indoors during the winter. Outside of the breeding season these lively little birds are quite contented to be with other birds in an aviary. (For food, see the fire finch.)

Orange-cheeked waxbill *(Estrilda melpoda)*

Just as well suited and pleasant to keep is this somewhat smaller bird than the grey waxbill. It comes from West Africa and can be crossed with the grey waxbill. Both sexes look alike, but the female is a bit duller in color. They sing their pleasant little song the whole day through, but this is often difficult to hear in an outdoor aviary because it is so very soft. However, this changes drastically during the mating and breeding season, at which time the male lets out shrill warning and call-notes. Treat as you would the grey waxbill.

Cuban finch *(Tiaris canora)*

This finch comes from Cuba. As long as the male is "single," he has a belligerent nature, but as soon as he gets a "wife" he becomes less quarrelsome. These birds are especially well suited for large aviaries housing other birds. They breed very well as long as they have live foods such as fresh ant eggs, insects, etc. They lay four to seven eggs in a pouch-shaped nest. They also have the habit of pushing other birds out of their nests and annexing these onto their own! Therefore it is recommended that Cubans be housed with bigger birds if you do not want to discover, sooner or later, abandoned clutches of eggs. The Cubans like peace and quiet for themselves during the breeding season, so I would advise you not to check their nests if you want the breeding to go through without incident. Feed like the green singing finch.

Olive finch *(Tiaris olivacea)*

The olive finch does not have the vivid yellow cheek spot so characteristic of the little Cuban finch. The olive finch comes from southern Mexico, Cuba, Haiti, Jamaica and some of the other West Indian islands. This large finch is less quarrelsome than the smaller Cuban and can be kept peacefully in an aviary with zebra finches and other strong birds. They breed well when provided regularly with live insects and such. Do not house the olive finch with the small Cuban finch for then the chance of successful breeding is negligible.

Red-cheeked cordon-bleu *(Granatina bengala)*

The well-known red-cheeked cordon-bleu comes from Central Africa. It is easy to tell the male from the female for the female lacks the red cheek spot and is a much duller color. They are very pleasant little birds, always keeping themselves busy. After they become accustomed to their surroundings, they are not easily upset. Their nest looks very much like that of the orange-cheeked waxbill. Both male and female alternate the brooding of the four to six eggs (sometimes more). The presence of a number of couples in one aviary stimulates brooding considerably.

Green singing finch *(Serinus mozambicus)*

This species, from Central Africa, is most desirable for its song. It likes to use canary nests for brooding, but it also builds a cup-shaped "cradle" in a thicket. After a breeding time of 13 to 14 days, the young hatch and remain in the nest for three to three and a half weeks. Then the father takes upon himself the care of the offspring. As soon as the young can fend for themselves they must be housed separately so that the parents can begin with a new clutch. Along with canary seed they eat greens, ant eggs, mealworms, universal food and canary egg mixture.

Grey singing finch *(Serinus leucopygius)*

This grey singing finch comes from Africa and, as its name implies, it is an extraordinary singer. Its song makes up for what it lacks in color. Both male and female quickly build their cup-shaped nest, but the female takes care of the breeding and the young. As soon as the offspring are grown they must be taken away from the parents. The grey singing finch is a very strong bird, and if a few drops of cod-liver oil (three drops to a kilo) are added to the seed the female will not succumb to egg-binding.

Bengalese *(Uroloncha domestica)*

Our last bird is the extremely well known Bengalese, which requires the same sort of care as the zebra finch. This bird is not found in the wild but was bred from a long-tailed brown mannikin male and a striped brown mannikin female. There are already a number of varieties such as the pure white, beige-white, brown flecked and so forth. There are also crested varieties that are quite desirable for exhibitions and judgings, but we will not give the heredity chart of this breed here. The sexes cannot be differentiated, but the song of the male is a sure way of identifying him. They require fresh bath water daily, and cod-liver oil and cuttlebone are very good for them. They are excellent foster-parents! Whenever we put eggs from a different kind of bird in the breeding nest of the Bengalese, it will accept them and brood them. Finally, it may be superfluous but nonetheless useful to call your attention to the following: remember that throughout the year the birds require *fresh greens* in addition to their regular daily diet of seed and fruit. Also do not forget to give them fresh drinking and bath water every day.

Index

(Pages set in *italic* type refer to illustrations.)